How Justice Is Served

Jed Kurzban

How Justice Is Served

Disclaimer

This publication is designed to provide accurate and authoritative information regarding the subject matter contained within. It should be understood that the author and publisher are not engaged in rendering legal, accounting, or other financial service through this medium. The author and publisher shall not be liable for your misuse of this material and shall have neither liability nor responsibility to anyone with respect to any loss or damage caused or alleged to be caused, directly or indirectly, by the information contained in this book. The author and/or publisher do not guarantee that anyone following these strategies, suggestions, tips, ideas, or techniques will become successful. If legal advice or other expert assistance is required, the services of a competent professional should be sought.

Expert Press

www.ExpertPress.net

Table of Contents

THANK YOU

I want to take a moment to thank everyone for helping me get my random notes and thoughts on paper and turn them into an outline, a manuscript, and, finally, the book you're reading now. This is not something I have done alone, nor was it a solo effort in obtaining the information I have tried to pass on. As they say, "It takes a village." I have been fortunate enough to work with my father, Marvin, and my Uncle Ira, who have *mostly* supported me, and my partners John, Helena, Kevin, and Eddie. And I could do little without my right hand, Lauren. Thank you all.

Writing this book has been a lifelong dream for me. Though I've read and highlighted scores of trial books during my career, I've never found a book organized in a way that I use the ideas I've detailed here. I hope "How Justice Is Served" fills that void.

Throughout the years, my office has been maintained by shepherding righteous clients, excellent staff, and top-notch attorneys to help foster the kind of atmosphere our clients deserve. My staff continues to rise to the challenge, making all things possible when it comes to serving and seeking justice for our clients.

Of course, I need to thank my wife and my unofficial editor, Evan, as well as my official editors and the staff at Expert Press. Please know I value the effort.

Oh, and thank you for reading this.

Author's Note

If you are reading this book, I think you will find it is intended for practicing attorneys or anyone who wants to better understand persuasive communication. The book does not offer legal, psychological, practitioner, or any other covert or clandestine techniques of persuasion. These are my opinions, musings, and thoughts alone. It does not take the place of consultation with an attorney or another professional with appropriate expertise and experience in the field of legal advice or legal consultation.

Attorneys are strongly recommended to evaluate the techniques and opinions presented in this book, relying on their own research, experience, and judgment. I recommend you be you when it comes to any legal tactics or discussions. Attorneys are also encouraged to consult applicable rules, regulations, procedures, cases, and statutes for any state they are practicing in, and any decisions about applying this book's information, techniques, ideas, and opinions to a particular case or client should be case specific. After all, that is the fun part.

Cases, discovery, pleadings, quotations from published works, and other sources are for illustrative purposes only and may not be the best approach for use in a case if you don't take the time to understand the case. These ideas and concepts are not secrets but are not always used correctly. Any idea or technique in this book was either invented by me alone or completely stolen. Kidding, but many ideas have been around a long time, and credit was giving appropriately, I believe. My ideas are my ideas alone, but many are based on those titans who came before me. After all, we are a small legal community and getting justice for our clients is the ultimate calling for us all.

Names of participants, litigants, witnesses, and counsel have been fictionalized (except where otherwise stated or directly quoted from published court opinions). Any similarities between these fictionalized individuals and entities and real persons are strictly coincidental.

All references to copyrighted works and third-party trade-marks are strictly informational and serve only as instruction and commentary. The author and publisher do not claim or imply any sponsorship, endorsement, or affiliation with the copyright or trademark owners.

The author and publisher deny any liability or responsibility for loss or damage resulting from this book's use and the ideas, opinions, or information within. Remember, you be you.

I can't promise this book will make you win every case, but it will certainly help if applied right. At least, I think so!

Introduction

Getting Punched in the Mouth

Here I sit, a law student working for my attorney father, and I'm listening to him give a closing argument in a personal injury case. The defendants admitted guilt on the first day of the trial but spent the duration of the trial trying to minimize the award they were sure to have to pay our client.

Now, my father is a gifted lawyer. He's a brilliant, creative thinker. And before we go any further, I need to tell you how blessed I feel to have been able to work with him — to watch how he operates and learn how he thinks and to have been inspired in my career by him and by other brilliant attorneys.

OK, back to the trial. Dad's up there, giving his closing argument and driving home the point that it's not about the money. It's about justice.

"Think about the injustice," he says (or something to that effect), "of making my clients wait years just to be heard. And now — now that the defendants are here in court, they admit they were wrong, but they don't want to make things right. They want to get away with the injustice of giving my client pennies for what they did to them."

I remember thinking this was a pretty good closing argument. But I'll never forget what my father did next.

He threw 100 pennies into the air, right there in front of God, the judge, the jury, the stunned defendants, and everybody else.

I'll never forget hearing those pennies crash to the floor and watching them fall all over the jury bar and the tables. I'll forever have the picture in my mind of how they glinted under the courtroom lights.

And, of course, I'll always remember the judge's apparent (and loud) dismay as he ordered my father to pick all the pennies up. (Needless to say, it was yours truly, the trusty apprentice, who got down on hands and knees to collect the coins. It was my first official chore in a courtroom trial — and I loved it.)

I remember being amazed at the theatricality, the utter *coolness*, and the unforgettable nature of this move on my father's part.

I was hooked.

§

I'm Jed Kurzban. I grew up in the richly diverse community of Miami, Florida, and went to law school at the University of Miami. And that day, several years ago, when I had to crawl around on the floor picking up pennies, was one of several experiences that inspired me to have a unique career in the practice of personal injury law.

I'm pleased to say our firm has helped many clients get justice (real justice) after they've been wronged by defendants who are most often interested primarily in how to make (and save) money. That's why, for me, it isn't about the money. It isn't about running expensive ads to get cases and working those cases to make more money to run more ads to land more cases.

There are plenty of lawyers who do business that way.

No, for me, it started with that penny-picking experience and other moments like it. I developed a passion for helping the community, starting with Miami and extending to a national practice, especially in medical malpractice cases. I've always said, "If I'm not home with my wife and kids, I'd rather be helping people."

When the "little guy" is wronged (often maimed) by a deep-pocketed entity that can afford to do whatever it takes to minimize damages, that's when folks like me have to step in to fight for them — to fight for real justice. Having a guy like me (one who's learned the hard way how to win over a jury, failed every way you can think of, and is willing to work hard and bring every possible advantage to bear for my clients) as their advocate is just about the only way the "little guy" is going to get justice.

This is important if you want to help the little guy. The judge is against you, public opinion is against you, and the largest companies in the world (insurance companies) are against you. It's an uphill battle, to say the least. You need to convince a conservative judge, educate a jury who has been lied to about our civil jury system for decades, and fight deep pockets that have used all their money and resources to crush your client.

I've noticed there are principally two kinds of personal injury attorneys: "business" attorneys and "advocate" attorneys.

Business attorneys run their practice like a business, with consistent advertising and marketing designed to maximize the number of cases they acquire and the amount of money they make. (I'm not knocking the business attorney. It's just not who I am.)

Advocate attorneys like me are probably a little harder to find. Because we're not in it for the money per se but for what the money represents for our clients; we're in it for justice, for the opportunity to be that person who helps the injured in ways nobody else can — for the chance to help David whip Goliath one more time.

§

I truly relate to the Davids out there, probably because I started out as a bit of a David myself.

I have to say, I struggled in law school. It was like I'd hit a wall, academically speaking, and at first, I couldn't understand why I couldn't roll up my sleeves and work hard to get over the wall. I'd been able to do that my entire life, up to that point.

Luckily, I had a dean who took an interest in me and had me tested for what she suspected was a problem with dyslexia. Ouch! She was right.

I had to take a semester off law school to learn to read all over again, starting with three-letter words and continuing on the most humbling trek through remedial learning you can imagine. (If you're reading this book, you probably know that if you have a hard time reading, you're going to have a very difficult time getting through law school.)

Previously, I'd somehow managed to outwork my severe dyslexia. Now, I had to work through it and learn to do great work *with* it.

That early failure in my meteoric rise to legal stardom (ha!) instilled in me a passion for helping people who struggle and can't understand why they aren't getting the results they should, whether it be for mental or physical injuries.

That goes for my clients, of course, and it goes for my colleagues as well. That's why I wrote this book.

My practice is primarily unique in two ways: My preparation is in depth, detailed, and probably second to none. (Thank you, Dad.) I've also learned through experience, both good and bad, that there's no substitute for creativity. *Like Popeye would say, "I am who I am."*

Let's talk about preparation first. A successful case starts with as much preparation as you can for the fight you're going to be waging. I never assume I will just settle a case for money. I take every case to go to the jury and fight for David. Of course, not every case gets to the jury.

Yes, it's a fight. As a plaintiff's attorney, you'll find yourself in a hostile ring with an adverse judge and jury who might start with the attitude that you're just trying to "win the lotto" for your client at the defendant's outlandish expense. And, of course, the defense team will be throwing every punch they can to try to knock your client out of their chance at justice. They can out-spend you 100-to-1 and have no compassion for the reality of the situation.

Preparation is essential, but it's only part of the fight. I'm fond of a quote by legendary boxer Mike Tyson, who said, "Everybody has a plan until they get punched in the mouth" (or something like that). I'm reminded of this quote whenever I'm working on a case for which my planning and preparation have been impeccable, but something happens that requires me to think on my feet and adjust things. And no matter how prepared you are, those things are going to happen. To be honest, it's my favorite part. As a kid, I loved to improvise and think on my feet. It is a gift that's hard to impart but a skill to strive for.

That's when it's handy to have creativity on your side, like the lawyer that one of my law school professors told me about, who helped his client by smoking a cigar.

It turns out this attorney ended up with a case involving a "bad client," one whose testimony would likely not be as helpful to his case as the attorney would like. In those days, one could smoke in court, so during the client's testimony, the lawyer made a show of lighting a huge cigar and puffing on it. At first, the jury didn't take much notice. They were soon distracted from the unfavorable testimony because they were watching for the giant ash on the end of this cigar to fall on the attorney's chest! By the end of the testimony, the jury had utterly ignored what had been said (the ash never fell!).

The attorney later confessed to a colleague that he'd planned the whole thing, including inserting a large paper clip into the cigar to keep the ash from falling.

That's a great example of creativity and preparation working together to help a client — even a client who doesn't do much to help himself.

When you have the advocate's mindset, you pull out all the stops to help your David get justice over Goliath. That's why I don't take cases for money. I don't want cases I think need to be settled. I want to creatively prepare for and work hard to win at trial — because that's how the Davids of this world get real justice. I want to make a difference in the world with my work and change the jury's conscience. If I can't do that, I don't feel successful, no matter how much money ends up changing hands.

§

In "How Justice Is Served," we're going to cover the three phases that make for a successful personal injury case. I didn't invent these strategies and tactics; readers will likely have heard of many of them and even used some. This book pulls together years of experience with many cases and organizes creative techniques into a blueprint for successful trial work. Yes, I copy a lot of other people's research, but I use the information like Frank Sinatra ("My Way").

In Part One, "Evaluating a Case," we discuss how to assess a potential case when a client reaches out to you and how to begin building and creating your case frame within your story and your theme. It also stresses the importance of case stories being as individualized as the case or client.

In Part Two, "Preparing Your Case," we'll cover the importance of truly getting to know your client, their story, and their case (and being able to adjust your theme and case preparation as necessary). Of course, you'll want to anticipate as much as possible the things that will come up that could change your case, including the punches the defense team will throw at you. Part Two covers these strategies in depth.

Finally, in Part Three, we'll discuss the most critical elements of "Trying Your Case," from selecting the right jury to winning them over with exhibits and strong storytelling. In this section, you'll learn more about driving damages, making solid arguments, and arming your jury with everything they'll need to deliver justice for your client. In the end, a great jury can deliver a great verdict, but a bad jury can kill even a great case.

§

The genesis of this book is a large, brown, leather three-ring binder in which I've kept notes from years and years of cases, big and small, successful and unsuccessful, as well as seminar notes from scores of seminars. In my opinion, the best seminar notes came from the American Association of Justice (AAJ) and the Florida Justice Association (FJA) seminars. "How Justice Is Served" presents these notes in an organized way that will help you avoid the pitfalls I suffered and allow you to take advantage of the things I've learned or maybe redefine how to use some of the techniques you are already familiar with.

But it's essential to keep in mind that you have to be yourself and adopt and refine the techniques that will work within your practice and your authentic self. You be you.

I knew from the start I was never going to be a "Hollywood" lawyer with movie-star good looks — that I'd never be the tall, chiseled attorney with the booming voice. I am who I am. And, as it turns out, that's all I need to be.

A booming Hollywood lawyer might not have known how to win this case:

I had a client who was riding his bicycle through town and minding his own business when he rode into a ditch left uncovered during road construction by a city contractor who hadn't properly marked the barriers after road work. The hole filled with water and looked like an even surface, not a two-foot deep hole. The poor guy flew over his handlebars, landed on his face, and broke his orbital bone. He completely lost his sense of smell.

The case went to mediation, where I had to make the mediators and defense attorneys understand the gravity of the client's predicament. About 10 minutes into the midday mediation, there was a knock at the door. The retired judge who was serving as mediator opened the door to find a person delivering a pizza.

"That's for me," I said. I quickly paid for the pizza and set the box in the center of the table.

You can guess what happened next. Everyone got a good whiff of that delicious-smelling pizza, the melty cheese, and the aromatic sauce and oils. You can probably imagine the aroma as you read these words.

I slowly opened the boxes, made eye contact with the opposing counsel's adjuster, and took a deep inhalation breath of the "pizza smell." I offered to share my pizza, of course, and I made sure everyone who wanted a slice got one.

As we continued, I said, "Just think, we've all enjoyed the scent of this tasty pizza. But that's something this poor guy from Brooklyn, New York, will never again experience for the rest of his life."

I knew I'd won the day. We ended up with an enormous settlement on a loss-of-smell case, and I wasn't surprised. I remember thinking: They're eating my pizza — and they're going to pay my client.

I had prepared the whole thing, timing the knock on the door to coincide with the precise moment in my opening statement that would deliver the maximum impact.

That's me. Some might think I won the day with a "stunt" designed purely to get money. But it's not a stunt when the goal is justice. Great lawyers never chase money. The best lawyers I've ever known always pursue justice, like the justice I got for this client who lost his sense of smell. His award was of the size that will likely keep that city contractor from letting a similar disaster happen to anyone else because of their negligence. Justice was making these contractors do a better job in the future and my client getting his sense of justice by being heard and making these changes for everyone.

I guess sometimes you've got to serve pizza as your justice — but with just the right preparation and a pinch of creativity. That's "How Justice Is Served."

PART ONE

Evaluating a Case

Chapter 1.

The Client Reaches Out to You

You won't hear my clever ad spots on the radio, and you won't see my smiling face on television or billboards. I don't advertise my practice. I don't market my services outside my webpage.

Clients come to me almost exclusively by referral — sometimes by word of mouth, always due to my reputation, and often from other attorneys who know how I work and believe my creative preparation and execution might give the client their best shot at justice.

Intake: It's Personal

I almost always do my own intake (sometimes travel or trial requires a little help). I know many other personal injury attorneys have people who do intakes for them, and that's fine if it works for them. But for me, what works is getting an immediate chance to get to know the client, hearing their story myself, and assessing how credible and deserving they are.

I ask questions, and, of course, I listen to the prospective client's answers, but mostly, I pay attention to how they answer. Are they searching for ways to "frame" their answers? Do they seem honest and forthcoming? What does their body language say? How do they make eye contact? Do they have family or friends to help them? What do they want from this lawsuit? (The answer most given is <u>not</u> money.)

I want to be the first person in the firm to talk to the prospective client. A lot of these things (the client's emotional state, how they respond to everything from the easy questions to the difficult ones, etc.) are critical factors in evaluating the case that a paralegal or assistant would find hard to codify in intake notes.

This is one of those lessons I learned the hard way. When I was working for my father, I did an intake for him on a fellow who had been beaten up by police. It was clear that the officers used excessive force. During the interview, I remember thinking he didn't deserve to be beaten up by police, but he certainly didn't come across as a likable, "good guy." My father took the case, having never met the client, and it didn't go well because he hadn't had a chance to really assess his personal story and demeanor before we put considerable time and effort into the case. We ended up getting less in trial than we were offered at mediation because we'd overvalued the case. And that was because intake notes can't convey the gut feeling you need in order to make the right decisions about a client or a case.

Another one of my cases involved a client whose injuries, which included a loss of cognitive ability, weren't easily reflected in the medical records. But I took the case because the client came across with great credibility and sincerity. If I'd made the decision on the paperwork alone, I might not have taken this very strong case. Seeing his eyes and how he and his wife spoke to me and hearing about their ordeal made me want — in fact, need — to help them. The injury was so deep inside them that when it welled up and out, you had to feel for them.

That's why I always do my own intake.

As the plaintiff's attorney — I always represent David, not the Goliath hospitals, medical groups, and insurance firms — I can't get it wrong too often when deciding whether to take on a client. Unlike our likely eventual opponents, I don't have an insurance company paying me by the hour whether I win or lose. I have to win. I have to invest anywhere from $100,000 to $250,000 to bring a case to a jury. And you do lose now and then (but it can't be more often than that, or your business is in real trouble). The case may not be all about money, but I also know I need to win money — because money allows the firm to take on the cases I want to take.

So I want to serve clients who need to win for the sake of justice. I want those righteous cases where clients aren't just attempting to "win the lotto," the ones where justice is sought and, frankly, demanded. That's why I meet with my clients and ask them why they want to sue. The most common response my clients give when asked their reasons for seeking my help is in the nature of "I want to tell my story so that this never happens again to another family." Because that's what it's all about. Justice served.

The Next Step: Send the Client for Their Records

Right away in a medical malpractice case, sometimes after I've decided to take the case but usually as part of that decision-making process, I ask the client to get their own medical records.

Why? As the case proceeds, I'm going to request those records myself, of course. But when the patient asks for them, it tends to ring fewer alarm bells with the doctors or medical records department.

And get this, about half the time, the "official" records I end up getting as the attorney have been altered in some way when compared with the records the client obtained. Hmm!

Doctors, hospitals, and sometimes even opposing lawyers will try to alter a patient's records to make it look like the defendants did everything they could do to help poor David, who now wants to take out his frustration on them at the way things turned out.

It's called "doctoring the records" for a reason! (Although, on occasion, the records may have been "lawyered.")

So, I want both sets of records. I want to use those differences in the trial. "Seems the doctor thought one thing before being sued but another thing later on." Pretty powerful.

I had a case here in Miami some time ago in which the patient had been tested for kidney disease — five times, in fact. And all five lab results clearly showed the disease. But the doctors didn't diagnose it, and (of course) they didn't treat it.

I filed suit (and a sixth lab suddenly appeared!). But this sixth lab was different. The first five had been typed up as these reports typically are, and all had been billed and ordered. The sixth, though, was comprised of handwritten notes — not by a doctor or nurse, but by the office manager who was the doctor's wife (as we later learned). It hadn't been billed or ordered, and wonder of wonders, it showed normal kidney function.

The result? The jury was not amused or deceived and awarded my client a righteously significant sum of money.

And I wish I could say this is rare. Unfortunately, it isn't. So often I am faced with fighting altered (doctored) records, and every time I prove the records were tampered with, my clients are rightly rewarded.

In another case, a patient underwent eye surgery and was supposed to have had an eye drop medication administered to treat corneal scarring. The medicine wasn't given, and that's right, corneal scarring developed in her eye. Of course, I filed suit and got the doctor's official records (a tome of about 100 pages!). I passed the report on to my medical expert and soon experienced an "oh-darn" moment when the expert told me, "I'm sorry, as I sort through this report, it looks like the patient did get the medicine." Luckily, the patient had obtained her own records, and (outrageously) these unaltered records showed the doctor had missed giving this medication. Once the record altering came to light, the indignation we all felt about this blatant manipulation led us to add a count for punitive damages in addition to what we were initially asking. The incident drove home to me the importance of having "before-and-after" records whenever possible for comparison.

The Client and I Are Partners

When I take on a client, I make it clear that we're partners seeking justice for their injuries. It's the client's life; it's their pain and suffering. I don't presume to share the anguish of the defendants' wrongdoing. But I do offer the client a partner to help them seek justice. I'm devoting my time and my (significant) investment, and I make it clear that I'm going to do everything possible to help them.

I also make it clear that they need to help me help them. For starters, I won't take a client that I think I can't sufficiently counsel. We are counselors of law for a reason, and I always try to appraise my client of the situation. As an attorney, I pretty much have to act under my client's direction, so I don't want a client who's going to harm their case (or my good reputation) by asking me to do things that might be considered unethical. First, the client must "do no harm" to borrow an ethical principle from the medical profession.

Then there are things the client needs to do to bolster their case. Beyond getting their medical records, I also ask the client to make notes. I don't want to generate too many official documents that might be subpoenaed. Still, I want the client to document their "before-and-after" story, detailing what they could do before their injury and what their capabilities are now.

Why? Because it often takes years to get the case to trial. And relying on years-old memories is difficult for anyone, let alone a person who's undergone a botched surgery or a failed diagnosis.

I also ask the client to help me find "before-and-after" witnesses who can clearly illustrate what the client was able to do before the injury and how they've suffered as a result.

Medical records, personal notes, before-and-after witnesses — these are all parts of the "homework" I assign prospective clients, usually before I formally accept the case. And if I don't have a good feeling about the client from the outset during that first intake conversation or if they don't even get the homework assignments done, I may reevaluate whether I even want the case.

Nothing Beats a Client's Gratitude

Three or four other attorneys had turned down the case of a 27-year-old Phoenix, Arizona, man with a new wife and small child. He was very sick for an unknown reason and complained of gout. Nobody wanted the case, not understanding that he was not just complaining. The man was in kidney failure, and the gout was associated with kidney disease. I reviewed the records, found the problem, and advised the client of his condition. He soon sought help from the Mayo clinic, and they saved his life — but not before significant damage to his kidneys was done.

It's hard to take a medical malpractice case, especially in states where damages are limited and families of those who are sick because of medical malpractice can't often collect enough of an award to pay for the case. In this man's case, his medical bills well exceeded $100,000. What's worse, everyone told him it was his imagination, and at mediation, his young wife broke down crying, saying that she, too, thought he was just a complainer until we discovered that kidney disease was killing him. Her guilt for not believing in her husband was immeasurable.

But I took the case because it's the kind of case I want. This was a "David-like" family of folks who had no one else to help them. And the opponent was a giant medical group that might well have perpetrated the same evil on another family if they weren't held to account. In short, it was a "justice" case without a doubt.

The gratitude this family eternally expresses to me is a treasure in my life. They were extremely appreciative right from the start — the day I first took the case — for having someone who would fight for them, win or lose.

Most of my clients are incredibly grateful for my work once we've won their case, and I'm so pleased by those expressions of gratitude. Even if the "win-or-lose" gratitude is more special, all gratitude is wonderful. It's what keeps me going. The family is able to live with some semblance of normality the money bought them, but they know they made a difference in the community, and that's the real win. Justice was served.

More than the money we make, more than the reputation we earn — it's this opportunity to help David types beat Goliath and get real justice. That is the foundational reason we do what we do. The world can always use more Davids willing to fight the Goliaths.

Chapter 2.

Create Your Case Story (and Frame Your Case)

Every case has a story, and it is vitally important because your case will be presented in connection with a cohesive, well-thought-out theme that depends on the narrative. As I said, no two stories are the same.

In my practice as an advocacy attorney (the guy fighting for justice for the Davids of the world), I've argued many cases with similarities. But I don't group cases together into a common story and then look for that narrative in each new case that comes my way. Some attorneys work that way. But for me, every case is different, and every story is unique, just like every client is unique

To find my case's unique story, I start by asking a prospective client a few simple questions:

- How did you get hurt?
- How did you get to the doctor?

29

- What did the doctor do wrong? (medical malpractice cases)

- How did the doctor's mistake affect you and your family? (medical malpractice cases)

- What does your future look like?

- What economic impact has your situation had on you and your family?

- How has this affected you personally?

- Where will you be 10 years from now?

You might be surprised at how often these simple questions (especially the last one) are <u>not</u> asked when other attorneys take on a new client and case.

And that last one is crucial.

For instance, it's easy to "see" (pun intended) what a person has lost when they've lost their eyesight due to negligence on someone's part. But not all losses are so obvious.

Sometimes a person loses a hobby, a meaningful career, or even a way of life tied to their identity and self-worth. In those instances, it's almost as if the defendant has robbed the client of their very reason for living.

I had a case in Key West, Florida, involving a Cuban immigrant who'd been a fisherman his whole life. It's all he'd ever done; it's everything he *was*. One day, he was out in his little boat, stealing lobsters from traps belonging to others (which, of course, is a crime). And he admitted as much. But I think you'll agree that the punishment he received from the Florida Marine Patrol didn't match the crime!

To "teach him a lesson," the marine patrol officer came by in his much larger craft and swamped my client's little boat, coming so close that the wake capsized it, throwing my client into the water.

It could have been just a lesson in tough love, except that the boat spun around, and the propellers of the outboard motor caught and severed my client's right quadriceps. As a result, he could barely walk, let alone fish (or even board a boat) again.

We told the story — every vivid detail — to the jury when we sued the marine patrol. And because the jury identified so strongly with my client's story, we won an enormous verdict. The jury just didn't feel the bullying and "lesson" that the patrol officer dispensed matched the crime of lobster theft. This was a story of *right and wrong* versus *shouldn't have* or *wouldn't have*. The punishment did not fit the crime.

Not every client's case meets this "You've-stolen-my-whole-way-of-life" standard. But if you know how to look for it, you can almost always come up with a winning story when your client is bringing a righteous case and seeking justice.

Frame Your Case With "Rules of the Road™"

As you collect the pieces of your client's story, you'll start to identify patterns, and that's the fun part. You can begin identifying the rules that can frame your case in an easy-to-understand way for the jury. I didn't invent "Rules of the Road™" (Friedman and Malone 2010) — I wish I did; it's a great book — but I call them "case rules" and use them in every case, making them case specific. Coming up with my case rules is one of the first things I do when I start working on a case.

What do I mean by "case rules"? They are akin to the traffic rules we all learned as we studied the fine art of motor vehicle operation. For instance, in this country, we drive on the right side of the road. Always. It's a fundamental case rule! More importantly, all our fellow motorists also understand and follow this rule, and as a result, head-on collisions are significantly reduced. (In fact, it's only when someone *violates* a case rule that bad things can happen!)

To put a case like the fisherman's in a tidy, well-understood frame for the jury, we must identify, describe, and drive home the case rules that the defendant violated. And, as with driving on the right side of the road, it must be something everyone can understand and would *agree* is a basic, immutable case rule.

The following seems like a reasonable case rule in the fisherman's case:

Case Rule:

*Marine Patrol officers
must protect the safety of everyone.*

Everyone can understand the rule; no reasonable person would disagree with it. In this case, the defendants violated this case rule by bullying and intimidating my client, leading to irreparable harm.

Now that we know the rule, and the rule is for everyone (even those violating the law), we can next establish a case theme.

But first, in another case that illustrates irrefutable case rules, a Miami emergency room discharged a young woman with a left femur fracture. The ER doctor felt the fracture would heal on its own with the use of a splint. However, the fracture was comminuted, meaning the bone broke into several pieces, not along a single fracture line. After my client's injured leg healed, it was 1 ½ inches shorter than the other leg, causing a number of back and leg problems.

A skillful orthopedic surgeon could have taken more X-rays, seen the pieces, and wired them together for a better outcome with surgery; instead, my client's life was forever altered.

Case Rule:

Doctors diagnose. They don't guess.

I think we can all agree on this being a very reasonable case rule. (Not all case rules are one line, but it is preferred. If a case rule is longer, be clear and concise.) Everyone agreed with this; they understood that the defendants violated this fundamental case rule, and we obtained a fair award (justice) for her and her family.

All cases are unique, but I've used this same case rule at least one other time: in the case of a Naples, Florida, man who went to the ER complaining of chest pains. He wasn't a smoker or drinker, so the ER didn't run any tests. Instead, they guessed that his symptoms were "stress related" and sent him home. (They didn't want to wake up the cardiologist on call as it was in the middle of the night.) The man suffered a heart attack and died the next day! As in the previous case, the ER had one job according to the clear-cut case rules (the standards of the medical profession). They didn't do that one job, and a man died.

The universally accepted case rules, in both cases, framed things for the juries and made their decisions easy. Now we add our theme and create our story. But as a first step, the case rule sets the frame or parameter of your case.

I can't stress this point enough: Every person to whom you tell your case rule must agree to it. If anyone says, "I think there should be exceptions," then it's not a good rule. (*Is anyone going to say, "No, I think there should be exceptions" to the driving-on-the-right-side rule?*) An explicit case rule will frame your case for the jury. Try to push an ambiguous rule, and you're likely to get an uncertain outcome.

If you're adept at establishing the case rules, you use them to frame your client's case, including damages, and defeat the other side's attempt to muddy things up with jargon or vague language in advance. Case rules for liability and case rules for damages might not always be the same, but both areas need to be framed.

In one case, my client had suffered injuries that led to cognitive impairment. I knew the opposing attorneys would throw all kinds of euphemistic terms at the jury, such as "some cognitive loss" or "cognitive impairment." So, early in the case, I made the jury understand that every time they heard the word "cognitive," the translation was "brain damage." This association was an anchor I set to help establish a connection to the rule to help create our theme. We have set up how to create case rules; now, let's add case themes. We will address anchors later on, but for this brain damage case, my case rule was:

Case Rule:

Any amount of brain damage is unacceptable.

Theme:

The defendants will label my client's injuries as "cognitive" — what they're really saying is that they caused my client's brain damage, but just "some" brain damage.

The jury accepted this case rule, and when the opposing attorneys overused the term "cognitive" (exactly as I had predicted), the jury heard what I wanted them to hear. At one point, the defendants' expert read a statement that included 16 uses of the word "cognitive," and I smiled and nodded at the jury each time. They all understood that the term was equivalent to "brain damage." And no brain damage is acceptable due to negligence.

Brain damage is profoundly serious, easily understood, and something none of us would want to experience. Using my case rules and then equating "cognitive" with "brain damage" helped frame the case for my jury in easy-to-understand terms — and acknowledge a case rule no one would dispute. Case rules, themes, and framing all go hand in hand. And again, I anchored "cognitive" to "brain damage," so it looked like the defendants were playing fast and loose with the words "brain damage."

Your Jury Is Ready To Welcome Your Case Rules

Another way to put this is that a good case rule will confirm what the juror already believes. If you say, "A doctor who sees 50 patients a day is in a busy practice," jurors will likely consider it to be a solid case rule, harkening back to their personal experiences of being shuffled through the doctor's office like wayward cattle.

Put yourself in the average juror's position: Here you are, listening as attentively as you can to what both sides are telling you, trying to figure out for yourself what logic you should apply to reach your conclusions about the case. You're looking for the facts, sure, but you're also looking for *decision rules* to help you figure out how to organize and process those facts into a verdict.

When one side (mine) gives you those decision-making case rules in a handy, easy-to-understand, universally agreed-upon *frame,* you'll welcome it. I've just made a potentially intimidating and difficult job much easier for you, the juror (of course, that last statement is in my head!).

Once I had a client whose infection became so severe that he lost his ability to walk. "But," the defendant's doctors claimed, "We did everything we could to help your client. We took 50 lab tests, and we could never find the problem. We had no idea it could be this bad!"

At first blush, this looks like a tough case. After all, "Doctors are heroes" is the kind of case rule that many jurors walk in with from the outset. And look at what these heroes did for my client: 50 labs!

But when you reframe the case using this case rule — my case gets a lot easier:

Case Rule:

Doctors are only heroes if they never give up trying to help.

I drove this case rule home, emphasizing that none of us would want to lose our ability to walk because our doctors gave up testing us after five, 50, 500, or 5,000 lab tests — no matter what those tests cost. Get an answer; don't quit.

In this case, heavy metal poisoning caused the damage (rare but not unheard of and easily tested for — if you run the test!). Now we combine rules and themes. My client worked as a sales representative for a medical company, so the doctor didn't see a need for or bother to run the heavy metal test. But what the doctor hadn't bothered to ask my client was *what* he sold: metal implants that he kept in his briefcase and handled all day when showing them to physicians. Somehow, he was exposed to heavy metals. Shouldn't this doctor have asked and run one more test? *Jury, did this doctor do his best or give up too early?*

Remember Those Very Simple Questions?

Lest you think I have a bias against doctors (I don't, only against bad ones who break the case rules and hurt my Davids), here's an example of a case in which I used my simple story-finding questions and case rules to get justice for some doctors who were victims.

Remember, I start with, "How did you get hurt?" followed by, "How did you come to be treated by this doctor?" and "What mistakes did they make?" et cetera. Well, in one case, a woman had been burned so badly by doctors trying to use a fat-melting laser device that she could never wear a bathing suit again because her wounds were so severe. The mental scars were much worse than the physical scars (which were severe).

Of course, I thought about suing the doctors — until I learned that they had been "taken for a ride" by the company that sells these laser devices. The device manufacturer had promised full and detailed training on the device's operation but failed to appropriately train these doctors.

Case Rule:

A medical device manufacturer has a duty to thoroughly train doctors in the use of their devices for patient safety.

Simple, easy (and who would disagree?). In this case, the manufacturer had provided a few cursory pointers, but nothing that amounted to a thorough training. They just sold and delivered the devices and left the doctors with little more than, "Here's the on/off switch, and best of luck to you!"

A standard law firm intake might have led to a case against the doctors, but by really listening to the burned woman's *story*, I was able to mount a much stronger case against the real culprits, the manufacturer. And all because I asked the simple questions: "How did you get hurt? How did you get to this doctor? What did the doctor do wrong?" I listened not only to the answers but to the story behind the answers. Then came the hard part, getting the doctors to meet with me. That took some time but was worth the effort. (Why doctors are so afraid of attorneys is still a mystery to me. I am not their enemy; I just want to uncover the truth.)

One More Case Rule of the (Literal) Road

Dig for the real story, use your creativity, and frame the case with your undisputable case rules.

My digging unearthed the real "at-fault" party in a wrongful death case in which a woman died because another driver's car crossed a wide, grassy median and struck her car head-on. Wrongful death cases are tough, especially in a state where damage awards to family members are so limited that it's hard to pay for the case itself (so be wary).

This one seemed straightforward at first. The at-fault motorist was insured, and her insurance paid up. She was out of the case early on.

But what I wouldn't have found out without using my tried-and-true framing questions was that the driver didn't cross the median because she suddenly forgot the always-drive-on-the-right rule.

She had crossed the median to avoid a ladder that had flown off the back of a Florida Department of Transportation (FDOT) truck, causing her to swerve wildly and lose control of her vehicle.

FDOT caused the accident — not the other driver! And one simple case rule was helpful in this case.

Case Rule:

FDOT has a duty to secure equipment so that it doesn't fly off trucks and endanger motorists.

However, I didn't stop there. I knew the defense and the jury might think the driver overreacted, so I attacked the defense head-on. My dad and I rented a car and a pickup truck and went to the local big-box store to buy ladders. I then hired a videographer to sit in the passenger seat next to me and record while I attempted to replicate the event one early morning during light traffic. (My father made us buy and wear bike helmets for safety while driving the rental. True story!)

Full disclosure, I started working with my dad (as you all know), and this was his idea. He tossed ladders out of the pickup truck, causing me to swerve (luckily with more success than the unfortunate motorist who hadn't known what was going to happen as I did).

No rental vehicles, assistants, videographers or attorneys were harmed in the making of this film ... but we repeated the "experiment" five times and created a compelling short feature which, when viewed by the FDOT executives and attorneys, led to a sizable award.

(We did cream the ladders pretty badly, but I owned those outright, and it was worth the loss. Remember, we were wearing safety helmets; please don't repeat this experiment at home!)

Following is the surprise case rule that we ended up using to great effect:

Case Rule:

ANY driver confronted with a flying ladder to their face would lose control of their vehicle.

It's a rule no one would disagree with — especially after seeing our film.

Sometimes you come up with the best case rules, the best stories, and the best framing when you <u>don't</u> believe your first impression. Use your creativity and dig deeper, and you might be able to turn a good case into a great one.

Chapter 3.

Build Your Case
to Your Theme

Ever heard of "Burke's Pentad?" It's a structure as old as, well, Burke (whoever he was). That's not the point.

The point is, if you go back to the ancient days of Greek tragedies and the like, you'll find they were structured in a certain predictable way, which helps inform the audience of what is to come and lay out a story. For trial lawyers, it relates to how you might organize your case within the *story* and *theme* you've identified.

It goes something like this:

- The Act — This refers to what's going on in a general sense.

- The Scene — This gives a more specific sense (the who, what, when, where, and how), all those questions that journalists used to love to ask.

- The Agent — Who's the "bad guy"?

- The Agency — Was the agent acting on behalf of another entity or an agency?

- The Purpose — Why are we here today? What are we seeking? (Justice is always our purpose; money is always the other side's purpose.)

Using Burke's Pentad to build your case to your theme might look something like this:

- The Act (what's going on in general) — A man whose whole self-identity was tied to being a fisherman has lost his ability to fish.

- The Scene (the particulars) — To teach this man a lesson for apparently committing a minor offense (why) on a certain date and at a specific time (when), the local Marine Patrol (who) intentionally bullied him by swamping his little boat (how), knocking him into the sea and ultimately causing an accident that severed his quadriceps and left him without the ability ever to board a boat again (what).

- The Agent — In this case, the agent(s) would be the individual marine patrol officers.

- The Agency — The Florida Marine Patrol (which may well have been derelict in their duty to train their personnel properly) is the agency.

- The Purpose — Seeking justice for a poor man who can never be a fisherman again is the objective.

Let's take a quick look at building each of these elements.

Building Your Case Using Burke's Pentad

By now, you've done most of the work needed to form the *act* (the general sense of what's going on with the case) by compiling the story — from which will emerge the case theme and structure.

You've interviewed (and truly listened to) your new client, given them some homework, and now you complete the act through the process of discovery and entering your initial pleadings.

Your story, case rules, theme, discovery, and pleadings will help the jury understand the act in a general sense. You want to make everything understandable and as clear for the jury as possible. After all, our cases are judged by a jury of our peers, which means these folks are everyday people (not legal professionals), so while you have to tick all the legal boxes, you must also use the tools of your trade to frame things for your jurors and make your case very plain to them. This is not as easy as it sounds and is the first major hurdle for young attorneys. You need to explain the actions in a way the jury understands, but you can't talk down to them. Find the sweet spot of common everyday language but be respectful and honest. Don't ever talk like a lawyer; talk like a person (see *drinks in bar* section).

You'll also need to set the *scene* for your jury with the words you put forward (in written pleadings and oral arguments) and with images to the appropriate extent. Sometimes a picture is worth a thousand words — and if those thousand words would be beneficial to your client and your case, bring the picture! We'll talk more about exhibits later, but for now, you should expect to make clear the *who, what, when, where, why,* and *how* of your case (the *scene*) using every tool in your toolbox.

When it comes to establishing the *agent*, you need to provide the jury with a bad guy to punish. It's just human nature.

Remember, we're telling a story here, and classically speaking, all great stories come with a hero (your client) and a bad guy. Without a villain, the end of the story might be perceived differently. The jury might agree that something unfortunate happened to your client, but they may not believe that anyone is worthy of punishment. And your award or settlement will reflect that.

For your client to receive justice, a bad guy must be punished so that they won't do this kind of thing again to some other poor unfortunate person. The *agent* is the face of the bad guy, the bad guy personified, but he or she might not be ultimately responsible.

Which brings us to the *agency*. Was your bad guy working for some big, sinister (and hopefully well-heeled) organization and possibly even perpetrating his bad guy stuff at the organization's specific direction? Alternatively, was the *agency* responsible for training this person not to be a bad guy and fell down on the job?

Establishing an *agency* is crucial. Look for a corporation or governmental entity that employed the bad guy and ask how they acted before the incident — and how they reacted after it happened. Your jury will want to know that justice is being served and that someone is being punished for the wrong done to your unfortunate client. If the *agency* lets the *agent* go with a slap on the wrist (or with no punishment at all), the jury won't be pleased. They'll want to dole out a punishment of their own, which will be great for your client.

But remember our *purpose*. We're not out for a win-the-lotto sack of money. We're after justice. (The other side's primary goal is typically to avoid handing over that sack of money.) So the punishment — even if it's only reflected in a monetary settlement that defendants are required to pay out — is a vehicle for making the world better by holding bad actors to account so that they are less inclined to commit bad acts in the future.

Why Are There So Many Lawyer Jokes?

There are plenty of lawyer jokes out there. Why? Because many people *hate* lawyers.

And what's the reason? I'll submit that it's because we are the brakes on a system that would continue committing bad acts indefinitely if left to purely monetary motivations.

We're like the disapproving matron who serves as hall monitor in the sorority house. Consider these examples:

- Did you know that babies' and children's stuffed animals were likely filled with cheap toxic fillers in generations past? Did toy manufacturers stop using those nasty substances because they suddenly developed a love for babies? No. It's because they were sued so often for so much money that it became economically smart to avoid these lawsuits by using nontoxic materials, even if those materials cost a little more.

- Remember the well-publicized problem with a particular make and model of car that would explode when it was struck (even lightly) in a specific area? Why did the manufacturer fix this problem? Why don't those cars blow up when tapped on that one corner anymore? (Hint: It isn't because the manufacturer woke up one day with a conscience that they didn't have the day before.) It's because the lawsuits they suffered made redesigning the car a sound business decision — even when considering the expense to redesign and retool the vehicle.

- Care to guess why 1) hospital policies tend to change, 2) training increases and rules are tightened, 3) hiring standards are improved, and 4) patient loads are reduced to manageable levels following successful lawsuits for significant medical malpractice that cite the hospital as responsible?

Yes, we're the watchdogs who bark for justice when Goliath wrongs David. We're necessary. Without us, you might get blown up in your car on the way home from your botched surgery, clutching the toxic stuffed puppy you bought at the hospital gift shop for your now-orphaned child.

But you do hear a lot about "tort reform." The government would like to put limits on the justice we can get for David because they have specific incentives to protect Goliath. You hear even more about tort reform when a governmental entity turns out to be Goliath in a losing lawsuit.

And you hear a lot of lawyer jokes. Don't be fooled; bad lawyers chase money and do unethical things to get cases and make money. No one makes jokes about lawyers who help change bad public policy. Or if they do, they aren't very good jokes. What do you call a lawyer who saved kids' lives by implementing a better chest X-ray policy? BORING!

Ethos, Logos, and Pathos (Not the Three Musketeers)

While we're on the subject of Greek tragedies (weren't we on that subject?), consider how you might frame your appeal to the jury by keeping in mind these three Greek terms:

Ethos — We derive words such as "ethics" and "ethical" from the Greek word "*ethos*." Generally, it's what society expects in terms of "good and right" versus "bad and wrong." You're appealing to the jury's sense of ethos when you frame your case within established common societal values.

Logos — Here, we find the root of the word "logic," and "*logos*" represents the logical sense your case needs to make to the jury. It's an appeal to the jury's intellect. Think of it this way: *Ethos* governs "right versus wrong" or "good versus bad" from a values perspective. *Logos* represent "correct versus incorrect" from a logical perspective. For instance, we expect everyone to obey certain case rules, and when those rules are demonstrably broken, the logic of the case is clear.

Pathos — We get a lot of our English words from "*pathos*." Still, for our purposes, the key here is to appeal to the jury's passion in every sense, which includes reminding them of the importance of every type of relationship: parent-offspring, spousal, sibling, you name it.

Our sense of *ethos* might tell us something is wrong in a general way, while *pathos* would further tell us that the type of "wrong" that takes away a person's passion for life is very wrong in a specific and personal way.

It's *pathos* that tends to govern a jury's assessment of "pain and suffering" (which are not the same thing). For example, our fisherman's quadriceps injury caused him pain. The loss of his ability to fish or even board a boat — the permanent end to that activity from which he derived his entire self-identity and passion for life — caused him real and lasting suffering.

An example of how these three nonmusketeers work together comes from a case I found myself arguing against a Japanese car company. You may know that cars used to be made of heavy-duty, high-grade steel with solid metal supporting frames, but this company (and most others) discovered that low-priced, less durable steel without a solid frame made for a much lighter and cheaper-to-manufacture vehicle.

In this case, my client was a beautiful young dancer at the New World School of the Arts with a promising career that would hopefully (and did) include appearances on Broadway. Her career essentially ended when the car she was a passenger in (yes, a light, cheap vehicle made by the defendant company) struck a utility pole. The car folded like an accordion, and the pole easily penetrated the flimsy rocker panel, severing my client's leg. I had a metallurgist testify that the rocker panel was cents cheaper to make than it would've been with the kind of high-grade steel — the kind that the car company swore it used in its plans to the U.S. government — that might well have saved my client's leg, career, and entire way of life.

The *ethos*-driven case rule was that we expect car companies to make safe cars. *Logos* told the jury the defendant company had broken this rule and that they had wronged my client by using cheap, inferior steel. But *pathos* brought the case home to a very reasonable settlement after we demonstrated that the car company was willing to take the leg of a dancer with a promising future to save a few cents on a rocker panel.

(In the happy-ending department, I want to mention that my client went on to dance on Broadway, garnering rave reviews for her performance with a prosthetic leg that she would remove to wow the audience at the end of the show. But her mainstream dance career was over. The defendants took that away from her forever.)

It's Not About the Money; It's About Justice (Have I Said This Before?)

Speaking of happy endings, maybe cases like my dancer client's are the reason you've seen a large and growing number of ads on television about all the safety features car manufacturers are putting into their products these days. And here's a dirty little secret: Many car companies have gone back to using more high-grade steel in their designs.

My client wanted justice. And by using her story, Burke's Pentad, the case rules, and the three nonmusketeers of *ethos*, *logos*, and *pathos*, we got personal justice for her in the form of a fair monetary settlement.

Over time, with cases like these, we also get general justice for society as our Goliaths learn that it makes financial sense to straighten up and fly right.

Defendants in these kinds of cases often make foolhardy arguments to the jury when they howl about how the plaintiff is only in it for the money or that they're only suing their clients to "win the lotto."

I do a fair amount of work with clients who've suffered from undiagnosed kidney disease (shameless plug). Now, I should mention that diagnosing kidney disease is considered pretty "easy medicine" since the doctor can order a simple lab test to determine whether protein and blood show up in a patient's urine. If they do, kidney disease is present without a doubt. And if caught early enough, it's usually treatable, and the patient can continue to lead a relatively normal life. Left undiagnosed, though, kidney disease can wreck a person's life by depriving them of a basic and essential bodily function.

More than once, I've heard the "win-the-lotto" argument from my opponents in kidney cases. Everything from "Our defendants didn't know the plaintiff had this disease until it was too late" to "We did everything we could for the patient" to "The plaintiff lost their kidneys, and now they don't have to work; on top of that, they want a large sack of cash from our clients who are the real victims here!"

When I hear that nonsense from my opponents, it's a simple matter of asking jurors how much they would take for their kidneys. I say, "I'm an attorney. I do pretty well, and I'd like to buy your kidneys. Would $500,000 do it? No? How about $1 million? What are *your* kidneys worth?"

In some of these cases, the doctors even ran lab tests that conclusively showed the disease and its progression (but didn't bother to look at the test results). So when I ask them 1) why they bothered to run the tests if they weren't going to look at the results, 2) whether they might have done so solely to make the $15 for the test, and 3) if they actually expected the jury to believe they had done "everything they could" for my client ... well, you can probably guess the outcome we usually get.

Justice. Personal justice for my client, in the form of a high enough award or settlement to make a meaningful difference in the life they have left. And general justice for all of us, as these doctors won't make those kinds of mistakes again and won't harm anyone else in that way.

Maybe it doesn't sound like much, but over time, doctors become more careful (and better trained) because of righteous cases like these. Hospitals institute more safeguards and safety procedures, and insurers pay closer attention to doing what it takes to avoid big payouts in the future.

And everyone tells more lawyer jokes. But that's OK. We can take it. The joke is on them. We are making a difference.

PART TWO

Preparing Your Case

Chapter 4.

Adjust Your Theme
as Needed

We've covered some excellent tools you can use to build a solid story and case theme for your client in an effort to get justice for David in his battle with Goliath.

Sometimes, though, even the most well-built case theme needs to be adjusted to account for the fact that people (even the smartest ones) often process information and make decisions based on what their reptilian brain tells them.

People will say they believe something — but their actions, behaviors, and decisions tell you they really don't believe it (or don't believe it very strongly).

That is the sort of "reptilian thinking" explored in books and lectures by attorney Don Keenan and jury consultant Dr. David Ball (Ball and Keenan 2013). If you haven't read their books or heard them speak, I highly recommend their work.

In case you don't quite agree that "reptilian thinking" is a real thing, consider the reaction many young people had to the horrible COVID-19 pandemic in 2020. They'd say that COVID-19 was dreadful and that every precaution should be taken to protect vulnerable people who could die if they contract the virus.

But in many cases, people's actions belied their "beliefs." Even younger people who lived with elderly and susceptible relatives continued going to parties, hanging out at the beach, celebrating spring break, failing to "social distance," and taking a somewhat haphazard and careless approach to mask wearing — despite being told how dangerously infectious the virus was.

In this scenario, a typical person might say they believe "every precaution should be taken." (After all, to believe otherwise would be socially unacceptable.) But, in practice, this person doesn't take all of those precautions themselves — so do they really believe it?

Put differently, the person's logical brain would agree that COVID-19 was extremely dangerous and highly infectious. Still, their lizard brain might suggest something like this: *Yeah, coronavirus is bad, but it only kills old people and other people who have underlying conditions and were probably gonna die anyway. We all gotta die someday. Which way to the beach?!"*

When representing a client, you have to account for reptilian thinking and adjust your case theme accordingly. Fail to do so at your own peril and at the risk of losing your case (and justice for David).

I'm always on the lookout for potential reptilian thinking on the part of my jurors. An example is a case I argued in which a doctor's malpractice had caused a 6-week-old baby's death.

Here's how I uncovered what the lizard brain was likely to suggest to my jurors: I held focus groups and mock trials with groups of people who would probably "mirror" the actual jury's reaction. I presented my case story and theme and then paid very close attention to these "mirror jurors'" reactions.

I realized I was up against a few common beliefs that people bring to their work as jurors, including the previously mentioned notion that "Doctors are heroes." And when I laid out my strong case that the doctor's actions had ultimately led to the baby's death, I was surprised to hear this question from my focus groups: "Well, what did the parents do wrong?"

In other words, the logical brain was agreeing that it was sad that a baby died and that the doctor could have been a better hero. But the lizard brain was suggesting that it was less the doctor's fault than it was the fault of the baby's parents!

It was valuable to uncover this underlying, ever-present reptilian thinking. Knowing what the jurors would likely be thinking allowed me to anticipate that unasked question. In the trial, I was able to detail the painstaking efforts the parents took to nurture the baby — all the visits to pediatricians, the extraordinary efforts to find just the right formula, the frequent medical help they sought, et cetera.

I wanted to answer the question, "What did the parents do?" before it was asked. Because people rarely voice their reptilian thinking, I knew the likelihood was that the question wouldn't be asked at all — except in the minds of the jurors.

Unspoken Codes: The "Bike Lock" on Your Jury

The concept of reptilian thinking tells us that jurors will likely operate, to some extent, based on their underlying "coded" beliefs and opinions. You absolutely must figure out and appeal to these codes to successfully win justice.

Remember the combination lock you used to secure the chain around your bike when you were a kid? Well, these reptilian codes are a lot like that. You have to figure out the combination to unlock the real, underlying, and always-unspoken beliefs that might contribute significantly to your jury's decision-making process.

While you're at it, if you can create and embed a helpful new code into your jurors' minds, you make your case theme much stronger.

I had a case involving a well-liked, highly regarded client, a large guy who had worked as a bouncer at a popular local club. This fellow was so well thought of that the club designated a "memorial stool" at the front door in his honor after he died.

And how did he die? He died in a hospital emergency room of a nosebleed.

Yes, he waited so long for treatment that he lost a massive amount of blood. When the ER staff finally saw him, the doctors tried administering medical-grade cocaine to his nose in an effort to stop the bleeding, but it was too late.

Remember, many jurors enter with the idea (the code) that "Doctors are heroes." So, I had to drive home a new code that could at least compete with that one.

New Common Code:

Doctors may be heroes, but hospitals are nothing more than "processing plants."

Take a number. Get in line. Good luck. If you survive long enough, we'll process you when it's your turn.

You have to anticipate and address your jury's reptilian codes, beliefs your jurors will rarely voice, in many cases because they know some views are not socially acceptable.

Example #1:

Lizard brain: *Women drivers tend to overreact.*

Logical brain: *Shut up! I'm not allowed to say something like that! (Just pay attention when driving.)*

Brilliant attorney (you): "Ladies and gentlemen, let me show you this video of ladders flying off the back of a truck and ask you to ask yourself how quickly you or anyone would be able to respond if you had been driving the car behind this truck."

Example #2:

Logical brain: *I see evidence that the truck driver may have been at fault in a serious accident when struck on the side of the road by a tow truck.*

Lizard brain: *Yeah, but he's obviously an idiot to be on the side of the road.*

Brilliant attorney (you): He was told to be there by the car dealership and didn't want to lose his job. He complied and lost his life, but we added another defendant.

In other words, it isn't what the juror says (which will come from their logical brain). It's what they believe — their underlying code, direct from their lizard brain — that will probably rule the day when they enter deliberations on your case.

A person familiar with your personal injury case might say, "Oh, you were hurt, that's too bad. I feel sorry for you." But their lizard brain might be whispering: *Oh, you got hurt. Good for you. You just won the lotto!*

Sometimes, They Change the Combination

Codes can change, too, as society's common beliefs change.

If you think people tend to believe that "Doctors are heroes," what about firefighters, police officers, and other first responders?

Since the tragedy of 9/11, media and other companies have invested quite a bit in establishing the code that says, "First responders are heroes." And many first responders are truly heroic.

But, as we learned in 2020 from horrible events that ended up sparking riots and urban violence, some first responders behave in a manner that is far from heroic.

Bottom line: Always be on the lookout for changes in what will likely be reptilian codes in the minds of your jurors, based on shifts in society and popular media narratives.

Cures for Five Common Codes

In personal injury and medical malpractice cases, there are some common reptilian codes you should watch out for (and know how to address).

These codes are things your jurors are likely to believe but never express. Jurors come into the courtroom expecting certain things, and you ignore those underlying codes at great risk to your case (and your David).

First, jurors want accountability and personal responsibility on the part of everyone, especially your client.

Your opponents will undoubtedly argue that their clients (Goliath) are not solely responsible for the bad thing that happened to your unfortunate client. After all, couldn't David have done a better job avoiding this calamity? In fact, wasn't David mostly to blame or all to blame?

If your client did do something wrong, you need to address it before the other side brings it up. If your client was stealing lobsters, for instance, you need to cop to it, get it out there, and demonstrate that you want everyone to be held to account, including the defendant(s) — and that justice depends on it.

In other words, the cure is to anticipate this common code in your jurors' minds and give them a reason to agree with you based on that code. You can say, "Sure, David takes personal responsibility for his part of the problem. Now, speaking of personal responsibility, get a load of what Goliath is trying to get out of taking responsibility for!"

Second, juries don't like to see plaintiffs suing solely for money, and they likely have an incoming bias that your client is doing just that.

The cure for this common code is often something like the what-are-*your*-kidneys-worth argument I mentioned earlier. In all cases, you must make it clear that while you're seeking money for your client, the money is only part of the larger justice David is seeking (and entitled to). You also want to see the bad guys punished, the agency's policies changed, a new law enacted — whatever would constitute real justice and a change for the better in our society.

The third common code is related to the previous: Jurors are generally suspicious of plaintiffs. Why? Because all kinds of corporations (especially insurance companies) have spent large sums of money convincing the public that lawsuits like yours are "frivolous" or "ridiculous" and that it's all about the money. For that reason, your juror might enter the courtroom suspicious of your David and with an unspoken (but real) belief that your case is not sincere.

Your client's story is often beneficial in curing this common code. You'll want to show how your client is a real flesh-and-blood person (just like the average juror) who's just trying to get along in life. A businessperson. A homemaker. A mechanic. Just a "normal" person — definitely not the "professional plaintiff" your juror's lizard brain might be inclined to see.

Fourth, jurors don't like "victimhood." They don't see themselves as victims and don't want to see others that way. And they don't reward any sense that your client is a person with a "victim mentality."

This principle is related to "confirmation bias"; a woman died because she was struck head on by a car that crossed the median. The driver of that car was a woman, confirming the lizard-brain bias that women tend to overreact. The cure was putting the jurors in the driver's seat and demonstrating for them that anyone might have reacted the same way to the flying ladders.

In other words, I had to make the case real and personal to the jurors without giving them a sense that I was "blaming" them for their common code. I had to make it clear that we weren't playing the "victim card" but that the Department of Transportation had ultimately caused the accident, and what we really wanted was justice (a change in policy).

The fifth common code you'll likely encounter is the famous "shit-happens" bias.

I had a case in Hawaii in which a 17-year-old girl died of cancer. And my opponents were doing their best to embed this code in the minds of the jurors: "Cancer is a death sentence. It's tragic, but shit happens."

In other words (and related to the victimhood bias), the defendants wanted the jury to believe that we were playing the "victim card" and seeking cash for a death that, sad as it was, was simply inevitable: You get cancer; you die.

To combat this one, I had to make it clear that the doctors had misdiagnosed the girl's cancer and that it wasn't a death sentence until that misdiagnosis. Once her cancer became pervasive, medical science couldn't help her. However, if the doctor had made the right diagnosis early enough, the girl would have lived.

In other words, yes, shit happens — but in this case, it didn't have to happen. The doctor's malpractice caused the girl's death by delaying the diagnosis. The delay was avoidable, but after that delay, shit happens.

You Can't Win 'Em All

Do your best, and you can often anticipate, address, and defeat the lizard-brain thinking that might spell disaster for your case — but you can't win 'em all.

I had a case in which a child had suffered brain cancer and came to court with significant brain damage. As it turns out, the cancer wasn't diagnosed early but should have been. And if the doctors had made the correct and timely diagnosis, they could have treated the child's cancer without the radiation therapy to which they later had to resort. The child lived, but because of the radiation treatments, he suffered brain damage.

At the bare minimum, I needed to defeat "Doctors are heroes," "Don't play the victim card," and "Shit happens," as the common codes I was up against. And we did a pretty good job in the case, but I was ultimately unable to convince the jury that it wasn't a mere case of "shit happens," and we didn't get the right justice that day. The jury seemed to find that the family was lucky enough that the child had survived.

The good news is that this is rare. If you do your best and work hard to cure the common codes, you can defeat the lizard brain. I've won far more than I've lost, doing just that. But even one loss is too many, and I think often of this family and my failure to achieve justice.

Chapter 5.

Get To Know Your Client

Earlier, I offered some thoughts on the difference between a law firm focused primarily on profits and a firm focused on justice.

You'll remember reading about firms that run ads to get cases, focus on settlements and fees, and push for more money so they can run more ads to get more cases — ad infinitum. Spending the money and really investing in your case and client may not be the most profitable way, but it's worth it for the Davids.

There are big differences between profit-driven "settlement mills" like these and a firm that's laser focused on getting justice for the Davids of the world. And one of the biggest differences has to do with getting to know your clients well.

Those other kinds of firms do a great disservice to their clients by having too many of them. It's very hard to get to know 100 clients — no matter how many lawyers work the case. Profit-driven firms like these can never hope to really know and understand a client's story or who the client authentically is as a person. And, as I've pointed out, absent a strong narrative and theme, your chance at justice is significantly diminished. If justice and making changes in society (not profits) is your goal, know your client's wants.

A justice-driven firm takes a vastly different approach: It isn't about the money, except that the money demonstrates real justice for clients who can't get it any other way. These clients want to be heard and stop this from happening again.

I work my butt off to make sure my clients feel heard and understood and have a genuine chance to tell their stories. And I sure wish more attorneys had that mindset and took that same approach. Justice first, second, and third; supporting my firm — last.

Skeletons in the Closet

You need to learn everything you can about your client — the good and the bad. The more you get to know a potential client as you decide whether to take their case, the better your odds of choosing the right cases. (Remember, you can't get that wrong too often, or you'll be out of business.) Yes, it's about justice, but you still need to pay the bills.

To be a powerful advocate for your client, you need to know the little details about them, their story, and their case. If you don't get to know them, you might overlook some "skeletons in the closet" — ones you can be sure your opponents will not miss.

As I mentioned earlier, I always make it clear to my new clients that 1) we're partners, 2) I'm investing heavily in their case, and 3) they need to do their part to get justice — just as I promise to do mine.

For instance, let's say I had a case in which my client assured me their injuries precluded them from doing any hard labor, such as lifting and carrying heavy items. If the opposing counsel were to show a video they captured just days before the trial that clearly showed my client doing that kind of work, it would be devastating!

Though that kind of thing doesn't happen very often in my practice, once, during case prep, I discovered that my client had filed a disability claim eight months before having the surgery he claimed to be the cause of his disability. To say that made things more challenging is an understatement. Luckily, with my digging and talking to the client, we were able to explain the disability claim. Although it overlapped his new work, it was different work and paid much more money than his new job (which he lost because of the surgery).

I make it a point to tell my clients that the opposing side will likely spy on them. If they are caught on video doing things they claimed they couldn't do, there's no way we can get the best outcome (or even a good one) in most cases. The Goliaths will get every medical record and investigate whether the client ever complained before or took medications prior to the injury. You can't hide those facts, so find out what they've done, and be prepared.

I do my best to illustrate to new clients what we're up against when it comes to trials of these types, explaining the many biases and "common codes" we'll have to overcome. I prepare them for the unbalanced nature of the "boxing ring" we're about to enter together. As I've said many times, jurors and judges have negative assumptions about plaintiffs before their attorneys utter a single word!

Jurors (and even many judges) often see my role as the plaintiff's attorney as a "referee" and think my job is to come up with a neutral, unbiased position. Nonsense! My job is to be a powerful advocate for my Davids. I know the judge and jury don't like my client for the simple fact that he brought a suit for injuries. I fight for the Davids. Judges don't like it, the Florida Bar Association discourages real advocacy under the guise of legal professionalism, and legislatures want to stop my kind of advocacy altogether. But I'm fighting for the Davids, and it's worth getting their stories before a jury, despite these giant and appalling roadblocks. Never stop fighting until you get justice.

One way I advocate for my clients is that I ask them to provide reliable "before-and-after" witnesses who can testify in court on their behalf. These witnesses can attest to what my client could do before the injury and how the defendant's wrongdoing affected those capabilities. Let me tell you, they can really make a difference.

When a client responds to that request with, "Here's my brother. He's willing to testify, and that's all I can think of," you can tell right away that something may well be amiss.

The best clients bring a list of 15 great witnesses and say something like, "I know you only asked for three or four, so I'm struggling with which ones of these I should suggest we use." (That is how a partner behaves!)

And that's why I always tell clients there are two people they should always be completely honest with: their priest and their lawyer. Even if you lie to your spouse or children, you must *never* lie to your attorney. As your advocate, I need to know everything about your story and case — the good and the bad. Because whatever you might try to conceal from me will almost certainly be uncovered by our opponents at trial. Get in front of the issues and weave them into your story.

Remember my "penny-picking" apprentice story? Well, it was for a man who suffered a horrifying injury when a crane ball dropped on him. The impact smashed his foot and ankle and left him unable to walk (or even move much).

At trial, the opponents played a video that clearly showed my client walking reasonably normally and even working on his car (including using his "ruined" legs to move around under the car on a mechanic's dolly). Naturally, it was devastating.

But the story had a happy ending. We located and deposed the videographer who confessed to splicing the tape! He had doctored the video to show a "scene" that differed wildly from reality, making it look like my client was working on the car when it was actually someone else rolling around on the dolly under the vehicle (because the client couldn't). Yes, this case is old, as we had a videographer spying, but just because technology has changed, defense tactics haven't.

Again, as is always the case when a lawyer fabricates false evidence, the jury was not amused. We won a hefty award that clearly demonstrated their displeasure.

My client didn't have a "skeleton in the closet" in this case, but the opponents fabricated one! However, there will be times when your client will try to conceal a skeleton, and you don't want to be surprised by such a thing at trial.

In another case, my opponents showed a video at trial, undeniably depicting my client throwing punches before the police beat him. Those 3-5 seconds of grainy video was enough to convince the jury that my client was something of a bad guy himself.

"Skeletons in the closet" is always a theme your opponents will use if they can since it relates to justice (and, therefore, to money from the defendant's perspective). Juries want to reward real victims of wrongdoing by punishing bad guys. So, you absolutely must, on balance, demonstrate that your client is a victim and not a bad guy without telling the jury that he's a victim.

Go into the client's closet and look for skeletons. Have they previously sued for injury damages? Do they have prior convictions? Is there a substance abuse issue or record of mental illness? Sometimes, finding skeletons in the client's closet doesn't kill your case — but the surprise when the other side discloses things your client concealed from you almost always does.

Do Whatever It Takes To Get To Know Your Client

Making an effort to honestly know and understand your client is the only way to discover the skeletons that might be lurking in their closet. It's also the best way to learn some of the most powerful and useful elements of their story and theme, which could get them real justice.

Learn everything you can about your clients. What support systems do they have? What are their family dynamics? Are family members doing things for the client that they can no longer do for themselves?

I had a client with prostate cancer who had a revision to remove the cancer, but the doctor missed the tumor completely, causing the client to have a colostomy bag for life. The defendants argued the "shit-happens" defense, saying that my client was an 80-year-old man with previous cancer. What they didn't understand was that he was an avid tennis player who played tennis every week with his buddies for decades, and missing the tumor took away what was left of his golden years.

Look for red flags. Do the client's parents eagerly look forward to testifying on their behalf, or are they reluctant? Poor relationships can make some parents bad witnesses — but good parents can make great witnesses.

How will your client come across to a jury? If they don't seem to care much about their injury or the suffering they're enduring after a botched surgery, how will the jury interpret that? If the client doesn't care, why should they?

What is the client's potential in terms of training or rehabilitation for the future? Take, for instance, a 55-year-old guy who's been driving a big rig for 30 years, and his undiagnosed kidney disease prevents him from ever driving a truck again. What should he reasonably be expected to learn or be trained to do in the future at his age and with his background?

Some clients are up for the challenge of changing careers or energetically transforming their lives and opportunities, while others are not (or can't achieve it). Chances are, you can't learn that from reading intake notes.

Here's something else you might not have considered: where your client falls on the generational band, especially when compared with the jurors' average age. Maybe you're aware that baby boomers tend to have a negative bias against millennials but harbor a positive feeling about people their own age. When you know your client well, you can help their story and case relate to the jury (and vice versa).

For instance, if I know that most jurors on my jury came of age in the 1980s, I tend to use a lot of '80s music to present my case. They love that — and every little bit helps. If you have a slide show or a video, add a little nostalgia music, and the jury feels connected to what they're watching.

Do What Profit-Driven Lawyers Won't

Do you know those lawyers whose faces you see plastered on billboards and TV commercials? Well, if you're chosen for jury duty, you might see one of them in a courtroom.

But you will never catch one of those lawyers darkening the door of an actual client's home. They don't have time for that; they've got 100 clients!

In my practice, I do whatever it takes to get to know my clients well. That means visiting with them in their home, and I go there without hesitation. I meet their families and have even shared my family with them to break the ice.

I had a case involving a lovely couple who I could only describe as "New Age." They firmly believed in things like auras, energies, crystals, and the like (and they had a completely righteous case!)

If I hadn't visited them at home, I never would have learned this vital aspect of who they are as people. And even though they believed in some things I might not necessarily believe in, I took the time to understand them and appreciate why they wanted things filed on certain "good-energy" days (and why other days were off limits).

We had a tremendous outcome in that case, far exceeding my expectations. I'll never know whether the energy and crystals had anything to do with the result; still, it was important to me that they believed it did. My clients were thrilled with their case's outcome and appreciated that their beliefs and traditions were authentically honored throughout the process.

Get to know your clients as well as you can. It's the only way to be their best and most influential advocate. And don't expect things to go well just because you file and argue on "good-energy" days. That said, ever since working with that delightful couple, I do keep some crystals in my window — just in case.

Chapter 6.

Get To Know Your Theme and Story

You've built a compelling story and a solid theme to help frame your case. Now it's time to do the deep dive — really dig into your story and theme and thoroughly test these key elements of your client's campaign for justice.

You'll want to know everything you can about how the story and theme are likely to play out in court <u>before</u> you present your case to a live jury.

The best lawyers know they don't know everything. They take the time to get to know all they can about the client and their story, the defendants (including ones who might be hiding), the precise actions all the players took, and how the case theme is likely to resonate with the jury.

Never leave your instincts or your creativity on the shelf. Look for more and better ways to check and test your case story and theme and find out everything you can before taking the case to trial. For me, the creativity is the best part.

You want to be a trial lawyer? Go talk to people! Talk to neighbors and friends and join professional associations like the FJA and AAJ and talk to them. Tell your story 50 times before you get to court. Think of creative ways to keep refining and presenting your story.

Establishing All the "Players"

Your case must make clear to the jury that for justice to be achieved, everyone involved in the story must be held to account for their actions (or their failures to act). Of course, this accountability includes your David, which is why you must do the up-front work to involve your client as a partner and get them to do everything they can to help their case.

Usually, it's pretty clear who the defendants should be, but sometimes, there are "hidden" actors who don't appear until you start doing your deep dive into your case story and theme.

Remember the case of the lady who was burned by doctors who ham-handedly used the "fat-melting" device? The doctors looked like obvious defendants — but a more in-depth investigation revealed that the medical device manufacturer was the real (hidden) culprit.

In traffic cases involving commercial vehicles, consider whether the company owners might be partially liable for the accident. It's a fairly common scenario. Sometimes the truck driver is solely responsible for your client's damages; other times, the driver's employer shares the blame if it failed to provide safe equipment or proper training or forced an unrealistic delivery time frame that can't be done safely.

As you dig into the story, you might even find multiple "layers" of defendants. The truck might be owned by a small company that is owned by a bigger one. And that ultimate owner might have cut some corners that diminished the safety of its operations. Yet another company may have been contracted to provide driver training, possibly cutting some corners too. You don't find these "hidden" players unless you do the right digging.

This was a case of a truck driver who delivered cars to a dealership. He was hit by a car and killed while on the side of the road delivering to the dealership. But it turns out the dealership forced him to make vehicle deliveries in that spot to protect their cars in inventory. The dealership may have been hidden had we not dug deep.

In medical cases, should the blame be shared by the doctor, the hospital, a medical device company, or another entity? Who may have contributed to the wrongdoing, and what potential defendants might be hiding behind the scenes?

How do you find out how your client's story relates to these hidden players? Here's a tip: Get ahold of the insurance bills and find out who's paying whom. You're likely to see names you haven't seen before or during your case preparation.

In one of my cases, this simple investigative step turned a suit against a doctor and a hospital into a four-defendant lawsuit, which happened to include a separately contracted billing company. The billing company overbilled the client, and to hide its wrongdoing, gave us a huge settlement to be released, still leaving the defendant doctors to be sued.

Dig until you're sure you've uncovered all the players, including any hidden defendants. Remember, when justice is the goal, your efforts must be aimed at holding everyone accountable.

Did the Defendant Catch and Treat Everything?

In medical malpractice cases, it's common to discover (upon digging) that the doctors found and treated one thing but missed something else. Often, that "something else" turns out to be much more serious than what your David had initially been treating.

A physician is required to arrive at a differential diagnosis when the patient suffers from more than one problem. Doctors must do confirmatory testing to verify their diagnosis, prioritizing the treatment of the patient's most serious issues first.

For instance, a teenager with a fever, a high heart rate, and shortness of breath seeks medical attention. Maybe it's just a cold, but she may have pneumonia. The physician needs to rule out pneumonia first because nobody dies of a common cold, but adolescents die of pneumonia with frightening regularity.

If there's any question about treatment, make sure your client follows up with their doctor. (You may have to direct them to do so.) If your client did follow up, did the doctor follow up on the follow-up? It's surprising to some people how often this doesn't happen.

In one case (yes, another kidney case), my client did a consistent job of following up, going in for testing every three months over three years. Each test showed protein in the urine, and each time, the marker for kidney disease was more pronounced than in the previous test.

The doctor claimed he'd tested the patient for kidney disease, which was true. *But the doctor never checked the test results!*

What good does it do to run these tests if no one reviews the results? As you might imagine, it didn't do my client any good at all. So this was not a failure-to-test theme but a what-was-your-job theme? Test and bill or diagnose and treat?

Do You Need To Adjust Your "Frame?"

Use the story and the theme to put your client's case into a nice, neat "frame" for the jury, making everything as clear and understandable as possible to help them come to the right decision for your David. Never assume your jury is dumb and don't talk down to them but make things clear and simple.

As you dig deeper and deeper into the case story and theme, you sometimes find you need to do a bit of reframing:

- Confirm that you've identified the right case rules, ones that align with what your jurors will enter the courtroom wanting to believe.

- Understanding and anticipating the jurors' confirmation biases, incoming suspicions, and underlying "codes" is crucial.

- Frame your case so that your expert understands what you're laying out for the jury, giving them everything they need to emphasize the right points.

- Frame the case purpose around justice. Lay out the act, scene, agent(s), and agency (or agencies) so that the jury can see the righteousness in helping not only your client but society as a whole (and themselves by extension).

- Juries may come in with biases and codes that can hurt your case, but they also inherently want justice, such as better health care and safer roads for themselves.

You'll recall from Chapter 4 my Hawaii case involving a 17-year-old girl who'd died of cancer. If the doctors had paid attention to what her tests showed, she might be alive today.

This poor girl suffered horribly, finally collapsing in her high school classroom when her hip bone gave up the fight and crumbled. And if you think you can imagine how painful that would be, multiply your imagination by any number you choose, and you will probably still not have a clear picture of the pain she had to endure.

You'll recall that the doctors had diagnosed her with cancer and that, as defendants, they trotted out the cancer-is-a-death-sentence-and-shit-happens defense.

As we dug deeper into the story and theme, we found that the doctors had failed to "connect the dots" in this patient's case, and that failure ended up costing her life.

They had taken hip X-rays that showed significant bone deterioration. (In later X-rays, the girl's hip bone appeared almost translucent, which means the bone is literally being eaten away.) Those tests, coupled with the MRIs that showed bright cancer markers in the same place as the bone deterioration, should have led any trained medical professional to connect those dots and conclude that the cancer was eating away at their patient's bones.

But the doctors hadn't. We connected the dots in court by laying one image over the other and very clearly showing the jury what should have been plain as day to the doctors.

When we found these different images during our case prep and subsequent deep dive, we created a new case rule and theme:

Cancer requires doctors to check and double-check test results as it can be a death sentence.

Remember, we're not talking about a bruise here. We're talking about **cancer**. In this case, the doctors hadn't even checked once. And knowing what their defense would be, we struck first.

Upon seeing the images, the results were clear to everyone. It is always imperative to know that your case will be viewed by nonmedical professionals and jurors who can be confused by experts. We discussed road maps, but now we are taking those rules and lining them up so everyone will see the end of the road before you even get there. Think of a runway in a courtroom.

The story and case frame have been established; you are simply waving shiny red glow sticks down the runway you already built.

Test, Test, and Test Again

A helpful tip to remember: You don't know everything, no matter how brilliant you are (or think you are) — *thank you, wife* — or how well you've prepared your case. Get all the feedback you can, formally and informally, so you can try to anticipate how your case story and theme will "play" in court. And listen to your instincts.

Often, once I've assembled a theme I'm pretty confident about, I'll go to a bar and approach four or five random people and say, "I'll buy the next round of drinks if you'll listen to my story for 10 minutes and tell me what you think." Yes, I really do this, and yes, it actually helps, but you need to find your own path for theme refinement.

No one has ever refused my offer. And it's given me some valuable insight into how "regular folks" (like jurors) will respond to my case theme.

I also hold more formal focus groups to gather feedback. Sometimes I present the case myself; other times, I have someone else run the focus group so that the participants don't know who's behind it. I've even hired actors to present my cases to focus groups to test a specific issue or theme.

You can never get too much feedback on your case story and theme before your trial begins. You'll want to get as many honest, arm's-length reactions as you can gather.

I had a case in Arizona where this proved to be a deciding factor. My client, a young boy, had been stricken with kidney disease at an early age. He also suffered from a growth deficiency. His doctors had treated him with growth hormones, but they didn't diagnose or treat the kidney disease.

Knowing from experience that one of the side effects of kidney disease was delayed growth, my instincts told me the child's growth deficiency was caused by his undiagnosed kidney disease. I was sure (and a little stubborn) about it!

But I took the time and effort to get as much feedback from others as I could. And I kept hearing the same question: "Isn't it possible that the boy had both diseases and that the doctors had treated one of the diseases fairly appropriately?"

I finally got it through my head that this was possible, and it's a good thing because this understanding helped me frame the case much more accurately than I otherwise would have. I ended up with a convincing story: The doctors had been so busy treating the growth deficiency that they had missed the kidney disease altogether — until much too late in the game.

Use your experience and instincts, but test, test, test your case story and theme and make sure you reframe the case when necessary.

Once you get the frame and all its ingredients right, you're ready to plan how to present the case to the actual jury. The ingredients are set out, the protein has been selected, and the pan is hot. Now we prepare the presentation and plating of the case. (Yes, I also love food, not just sports.)

Chapter 7.

Plan Your Case

All the effort you and your team have put forth so far will come in very handy as you assemble the pieces into a plan for how you will proceed at trial.

You'll want to gather all the evidence you can (covering all the categories of evidence that might be relevant to your case, as we've discussed) and start figuring out how to present that evidence in a way that makes it easy for the jury to reach your desired outcome.

Your expert needs to be part of the conversation. Include them. Call them. (Don't email them, as emails are discoverable.) Their contributions must fit seamlessly into your client's case.

And, of course, you'll want to do everything you can to anticipate the other side's arguments. They're also making plans, and it might not take that much imagination and cleverness on your part to figure out what those plans are likely to include (and to think of ways to "blow up" those plans).

Ammunition for Your "Blow-Up File"

As you dig into the case and gather evidence and information, you'll undoubtedly come across some real gems that can put your case "over the top."

Just about everything you gather will be helpful, at least as "background" for your case presentation. And some things you find will be downright "explosive" enough to help you blow up your opponents' case!

Very early in my case planning, I assemble a "blow-up file" to deploy at trial. And I'm using that term in different ways: 1) in the sense that the things in my *blow-up* file will help explode the other side's argument and 2) because I'll *blow up* (enlarge) critical information from that file to create giant exhibits that amplify those explosions in order to 3) *blow them up* for the jury!

For instance, I might take an explosive deposition quote and feature it on a foam board or an overhead slide. I use just that one page, one paragraph, or one sentence and enlarge it to a larger-than-life typeface for the jury to see. (I want my blow-up file exhibits to be visible from space!)

As my team and I gather evidence for our David's case, I'm always on the lookout for those explosive little nuggets that become ammunition for my blow-up file. It's such an integral and enjoyable part of planning the case. And you just can't underestimate the value of these things.

It's like the "little boy detective" part of planning the case: *Find the secret text. Track down the key passage in the medical record. Discover the other side's accidental admission of guilt!*

Leave No Stone Unturned

There are lots of places to dig for evidence to support your case and expand your blow-up file.

Not every category of evidence is relevant to every case. Use your experience, instincts, and creativity to make sure you've left no stone unturned in your search for "ammunition."

Of course, some evidence gathering will fall into the legal category of *discovery*, but if you're clever, you can find ammunition outside the formal discovery process.

For example, I had a case where the ER misdiagnosed my client and left him with permanent "white-matter" brain loss from a stroke they did not diagnose. The head of the ER was a physician who told me (under oath) that they had limited resources and could not treat the patient as quickly as they would have liked due to their limited resources.

The doctor was very nice and apologized for the fact that they couldn't have done more. A jury may have felt sympathy for the physician, but in doing a request for information, I found webpage data, including a video from that same physician, touting the hospital as one of the largest and *best-funded* hospital systems around!

The video went on to claim the hospital could treat everyone as soon as they came in, with unparalleled doctors and staff, and should be considered a system above the rest.

The marketing material made my "blow-up" file, and at mediation, the doctor hung his head in shame when I presented his testimony and the materials I found. My client's family got the justice they deserved.

Written Documents. All documents you receive in the course of your evidence request might be used to support your case, from pleadings and other filings to documents received in connection with requests to produce.

Sometimes, critical evidence takes the form of documents you <u>don't</u> find, as in the case of the doctored (literally!) medical records that included a sixth lab test — a test for which no bill could be found or produced.

I love using pleadings, too. It isn't uncommon for the other side to file pleadings that can be used as admissions as the trial unfolds.

For example, you might be able to cite a pleading this way: "The defendants admit in writing that they perpetrated this act as part of the normal course of their work." In so doing, you might use the defense's own pleadings to establish shared liability with an employer (that might have deeper pockets than the culpable individual).

I'm careful to include the "duty" the defendant had to my client in my filings — the duty the defendant failed to uphold. For instance, my complaint will assert that doctors have a duty to keep accurate records or that doctors with too many cases are overworked and can't give clients (like my David) the proper attention. Then, when the defendants issue blanket denials in writing, I can point out to the jury that they deny their basic duties.

"No wonder you committed malpractice, doctor!"

Depositions. An essential part of discovery is putting witnesses under oath in depositions. Some of the best ammunition for my blow-up file often comes from depositions.

If I can, I'll depose the truck driver and a representative of the trucking company. In jurisdictions where it's allowed, I'll depose first responders, such as police or emergency medical technicians.

If you're clever in crafting your questions, you can get some really astonishing answers in depositions — perfect quotes for your blow-up file. And, naturally, the best stuff often ends up in giant type on an exhibit that an astronaut might be able to read from space (and that the jury won't be able to ignore).

My team always summarizes depositions into files that make it easy and convenient to find information at trial. Even a smaller firm like my own often has an associate or two for whom this is excellent and instructive work.

Summaries are never used in the blow-up file, but a summary may make you question whether you did all of the follow-up you should have done. If not, propound some interrogatories and voilà; more blow-up material may come your way!

Site or Product Inspections. In some cases, it's appropriate to inspect a product or an accident site.

Remember the fat-melting laser case? I went to the facility and made a close inspection of the product — in this case, a medical device designed to use a laser to melt fat. As it turns out, there's a sticker on the device that reads, "Not To Be Used For Weight Loss"— exactly what they were using it for! (Needless to say, a clear photo of that sticker ended up in my blow-up file and was eventually enlarged as an exhibit for the jury.)

In a horrible auto accident involving the death of a young man, a highway construction crane was crossing the highway at night when the hook on its boom struck my client's car, killing him. The police report was unclear on how the accident occurred, so we conducted a site visit of the car in the junkyard. The pattern of destruction on the roof of the vehicle looked like a knife had split the roof in half. It clearly demonstrated that an object had gone through the roof, striking my client and killing him (and that my client did not die because of a rollover).

Demonstrative Visual Aids. In the case against the foreign car manufacturer that failed to use high-strength steel, a great deal of technical research and expert testimony was required to determine the precise definition of "high-strength steel." Would the jury clearly understand why the company's use of flimsier steel was such a problem? I found a goofy cartoon that illustrated what happens when steel that's expected to be sturdy turns out to be flimsy. It ended up being a very persuasive visual aid for the jury.

I love using timelines, too. A giant chart that shows the time-line of events as they unfolded can be very convincing, as was the case in Hawaii when the patient went in for testing 20 times in 24 months. The defense claimed they had tested my client 20 times, as if it was the case's dispositive fact. However, the time-line clearly demonstrated to the jury how often the patient had submitted to these tests and how many opportunities the doctors had to catch the abnormalities clearly shown by the test results.

"Yes," I argued, "You tested 20 times, but the results were abnormal in every case. What good is simply testing?" My fa-ther then used my 8-foot-wide chart and asked the doctor what the test results were for every test taken. After the first 10 or so "abnormal findings," the jury was convinced the doctor missed something.

The jury found the argument persuasive, and the timeline served as an effective demonstrative aid.

Research the Cause. Dig into your David's case to make sure you have a thorough understanding of the issues. For instance, in a medical malpractice case, the more you understand the medi-cine itself, the better you'll be able to present your case to a jury of your client's peers. However, don't fight with the doctor. You still don't know the medicine nearly as well as a doctor does. Think of an iceberg: Your total knowledge of the medicine is simply the tip of a monstrous iceberg, 95% of which is under the surface and invisible to you.

In the case of my young Arizona client who suffered from both kidney disease and delayed growth, my case would have been in trouble if I hadn't done enough research to understand the true nature of the connection between these two problems. One advantage we trial lawyers have over most people is that we like to use common sense to "connect the dots." A righteous case has righteous facts; don't run from the facts but embrace them.

Understand your need not only to prove liability and damages but causation. Did the breach or negligence cause the damage? This is the basis of most of the defenses you'll face.

Prep Your Expert. One of the most critical aspects of case planning is ensuring your expert can make the right points — simply and clearly — at the right time to support your case and the causation of your case.

There's absolutely no reason to keep secrets from your expert. You want them to know exactly where you're going with the case so they hit the right topics in their testimony or deposition.

Your expert will also be a valuable part of your research team. In the automotive case, I had hundreds of pages of technical details to go through. My expert helped us whittle them down to the main points the jury needed to know to decide in my client's favor.

In the case of my client who was supposed to have had eye drops administered, my expert first saw reports saying the patient had been given the drops. These reports raised a red flag, and we went on to find that those reports had been altered. Of course, you need to know the importance and value of the information, which is why you need to do the research and be prepared. Always be prepared!

Remember Mike Tyson

To paraphrase Mike Tyson: Everybody has a plan for the fight until they get punched in the face. So, a key to planning your case is to anticipate getting punched in the face.

I had a case where doctors had failed to diagnose colon cancer. They performed surgery to remove a tumor but missed the cancer, which then spread. Once they figured it out, they had to remove the patient's entire colon, requiring him to be on a colostomy bag for the rest of his life. Later, the cancer came back in the man's blood.

When the doctors' legal team presented their defense, they asserted that 1) this particular cancer was a death sentence, 2) it would come back anyway, and 3) their first mistake of missing the initial cancer didn't contribute all that much to the patient's eventual outcome.

I could imagine the jury buying this defense, so I had to adjust my case. I argued that the doctors' original mistake had made a miserable life far worse by forcing my client to deal with a colostomy bag, along with the needed radiation and chemotherapy. Hard to imagine a surgeon could make cancer worse, but they did!

I was about to get punched in the face, but I was able to counterpunch and show how the few good years my client would have had with his wife and tennis buddies were taken away. Even if you believe everything the defendants say, I argued, the years before the cancer could return had been taken away. Those years would have been that much more special knowing he was living on borrowed time.

What could the defendants say? They set this scenario and now they had to live with it. We were able to get enough money for my client to live the best life he could during the time he had left.

You have to anticipate the other side's arguments and plan ways to defeat those arguments whenever possible — but that shouldn't be your sole focus. You have to keep your eye on your own case at all times.

In the case where my opponents presented a normal sixth urinalysis, and my case was about to be blown to smithereens, we showed how they had doctored the records and forged this bogus sixth lab test. I had to maintain my focus on my case: A little girl lost her kidney because her pediatrician wasn't sufficiently trained to notice that her kidney was dying (as shown in the lab tests).

But Sometimes, You Have To "Go Rocky"

Speaking of Mike Tyson (and while we're relating your case to a boxing match), I'll add that sometimes you have to go all "Rocky" on your opponents.

If your memory of the many "Rocky" films is dim, you might think I'm talking about punching your opponents like a well-worn speed bag — but that's not what Rocky was famous for. Rocky won by being able to take punches without going down.

If I may quote Rocky, "It's about how hard you can get hit and keep moving forward. How much can you take and keep moving forward?"

(By the way, I have this quote on my wall. For real.)

In the case against the marine patrol in Florida, my opponent repeatedly argued that we were applying the wrong rules to the case, saying that there was one set of rules for the open sea and another for inland waterways. They continually asserted that we were arguing our case based on the wrong set of rules. Terrible, and it turns out they were right. These hits hurt!

Eventually, I had to admit that, yeah, there are two sets of rules. The opponents are correct.

I took the punch.

But I won by showing the jury, simply and clearly, that NO set of rules excused the behavior of the marine patrol — behavior that cost my client his entire way of life. My expert said so, and so did the defense's expert!

Neither inward nor open sea rules allow for the *swamping of a boat!*

The jury ended up disliking the way my opponent had wasted so much time on this technicality. And they arrived at a verdict that clearly demonstrated their disdain.

These are just some examples of how to plan your case in a way that anticipates the punches your opponents will throw.

But we're just getting started.

Chapter 8.

Prepare for Defense

The last stop in pulling together a strong case for your David is preparing for the defense Goliath and his giant army of lawyers will put up.

(Or, army of giant lawyers, in rare cases.)

As previously mentioned, the odds are against you and David — just as they were against the first David. You step into the courtroom, and already you're battling significant unspoken biases on the part of everyone from the jury to the public to the political and societal powers that be. (Even the judge is likely to dislike the cut of your jib — at least early on.)

While you should always maintain a focus on your case, properly preparing for the defense's case is a major factor that will, in all likelihood, contribute to the success or failure of your quest for justice.

One helpful fact is that the opposing attorneys might not be aware of all the advantages they have before the trial begins.

They might not fully seize every opportunity to play up those advantages.

But you must prepare as though Perry Mason himself will be opposing you. And as anyone who had access to a TV set in the 1960s knows, Perry Mason never missed a trick.

(Since that show predates me — except for reruns — I go back to Iron Mike when I say, "never underestimate your opponents.")

The Grumpy, Arms-Folded Jury

Recall the forces arrayed against you: everyone from the media to state legislators (and certainly lobbyists for big insurance companies) has invested significant resources to make the general public wary of plaintiffs in personal injury cases.

It's the "you're-just-trying-to-win-the-lotto" bias, and it's a powerful obstacle in your path to justice. In addition, years and years of tort reform has limited access to juries and access to adequate awards. By the way, "tort reform" is legislative talk for "We were paid huge monies by businesses and insurance companies to screw people over." Lastly, most judges come from big firms or state agencies, not small firms. They tend to be conservative to begin with and are usually less understanding of the uphill battle for justice.

Since your jury is comprised of members of the general public (who have been told lawsuits are the reason things cost more), you're likely to find them biased against your client from the outset. When was the last time you saw a commercial about a product that proclaimed lawyers were solely responsible for making it safer? I thought so.

(Side note: We attorneys must all do a better job of educating people about our role in society.)

But don't panic. You can overcome this obstacle using superior anticipation and preparation. The fact that you understand the problem (and know that you need to be better, sharper, and smarter than the opposition) is a great start.

I had a real David versus Goliath case in South Carolina that featured a military veteran who had been treated quite haphazardly by the medical personnel at the local Veterans Affairs Hospital.

There's no excuse for how they treated this guy. But what was the underlying reason for their behavior? Was the staff overworked? Didn't they care? Were they biased against veterans or older folks? Were they understaffed because of the hospital's rural location?

Again, there was no excuse for this mistreatment (despite the opposition's many excuses). But understanding the possible reasons behind the staff's lackluster performance was an essential element in our preparation and effort to resist the jury's easily anticipated initial "code" (bias): *Doctors are heroes.*

We worked to "recast" the drama playing out for the jury. In this case, the doctors had not lived up to the "hero" code and were recast — not as villains but as ordinary. Heroes don't make mistakes, but ordinary people make them all the time! In fact, we were able to portray the Veterans Affairs staff as mere cogs in a giant machine that was practically set up to mistreat veterans.

Our hero? The veteran, of course! My client. My David. And it isn't that hard to recast a military veteran as the real hero in our quest for true justice.

The "doctors are heroes" jury bias is pretty standard. In fact, it's almost universal, and it's an obstacle we have to overcome in almost every medical malpractice case. And while you have to be prepared to combat these common codes, you also need to be on the lookout for other biases that might be specific to your particular jury. If you know what to look for, you often uncover these specific biases during *voir dire*.

You can sometimes find these isolated biases during the initial testing of your story (say, by getting feedback from a focus group). But be careful: You have to do your testing in the same general geography as that of your jury pool. For instance, you likely won't get accurate information from a Miami focus group about how a South Carolina jury might be biased. (You're just going to have to go to a South Carolina bar, ballgame, or dinner party to get good answers.)

As plaintiff's attorneys, we have to be almost hyperaware of jury bias in all its forms, and we have to figure Goliath's attorneys will use this advantage to their full effect. It is important to remember that most defense firms and attorneys have been to trial many more times than plaintiff lawyers have been, and we need to outthink them as they have the money and experience.

You have to walk into the courtroom anticipating the grumpy, arms-folded jury, populated by people who start from a position of distrust and even dislike for you and your client. But when you unfold your case and watch the jury "turn" before your very eyes, it's almost magical. And it's fun!

Goliath Will Attack Your Expert

What's a good personal injury case without an expert witness? A credible expert is often indispensable when it comes to making your case for justice and your David.

However, what's a competent personal injury defense without a zealous effort to get your expert thrown off the case? Expect a *Daubert challenge* to your expert in every personal injury matter.

Rest assured, Defense Counsel Perry Mason over there will allege that your expert doesn't meet the Daubert standards. They will question your expert's qualifications or whether they are appropriately using tried-and-true scientific methodologies to arrive at their expert conclusions. (Just a side note, I much prefer "My Cousin Vinny" to Perry Mason, but it's hard to get much teachable law from him.)

So, it's critical that you challenge your own expert before the trial — in every way you can think of — and prepare them to withstand the Daubert challenge that's almost certain to come.

I represented a client whose doctors missed her breast cancer when it was still in its early and most treatable stage. The defense argued that, hey, cancer grows over time (there's a "doubling theory," which asserts that, over a set time, cancer doubles every X number of days), and the doctors did diagnose her cancer when it became large enough to be seen.

My expert had to make a professional "guess" about the tumor's size at initial testing. Of course, the other side challenged the expert's ability to accurately "know" what the size of the tumor would have been at that time. (Naturally, because the doctors missed the diagnosis, they never took an X-ray — so there was no definitive proof of the tumor's size when it should have been detected.)

Cases like these often come down to a battle of the experts. Does your expert's opinion "beat" that of the defendant's doctors or those of any expert witnesses the defense team calls? You need to thoroughly prepare and test your experts to ensure they come across to the jury with supreme competence and a deep understanding of the specifics of your David's case.

When the defense paints your expert as a "professional witness" (someone who's being paid for their testimony), it can be harmful, especially if the jury sees your employment of the expert as an "investment" in a case where you're just looking for a large award. Given the "he's-just-trying-to-win-the-lotto" common code that your jury's likely to start with, it can be tricky to get around this obstacle. But when your expert reveals he practices medicine, teaches medicine, and does review work only 5% of his professional time, how about that! You and the rest of David's team are back to being the good guys. Most of the defense experts are actual professional experts, and you must show the jury the difference.

In Florida, we represented a businessman who suffered from a terrible infection in his foot resulting from a missed diagnosis by his treating podiatrist. The lab tests were ignored, and the red and swollen foot was determined to be "healing."

Our expert, a teaching podiatrist, testified as to the emergent nature of the infection and the need to treat it quickly, as the foot has less fat and tissue than other parts of the body. The professional defense doctor testified that infections happen and taking lab tests is the best defense. Sure! If you bother to read and follow up on the labs.

I left the four labs on the jury bar and asked the jury to determine what should be done next or how the doctor should have reacted to what the tests showed. Of course, these people weren't trained professionals but average, everyday people, and they had no idea how to interpret or react to the lab values. As I explained, their inaction was equal to the defendant doctor's lack of response, and I left the case to my expert to explain what should have been done. The head nods from the jury box confirmed what I'd known all along: A good teaching expert can really help make a case.

Understand the Way Doctors Think

You'll be dealing with doctors in many of your personal injury cases (and certainly in cases involving medical malpractice):

- The defendants are likely doctors.

- The defendants' bosses at the hospital or practice group are doctors (or former doctors).

- Heads of physician groups at clinics or hospitals are doctors.

- Insurance executives are often former doctors.

- Your expert might well be a doctor.

- The defense's experts will be doctors.

- Opposing counsel, members of the jury, and even the judge might be doctors or former doctors or have family who are doctors.

Yes, doctors, doctors, everywhere doctors!

It's critical that you get to know how doctors think, so you'll be prepared for the manner in which a doctor is likely to respond to your questions and react to your case in general.

In medical school, doctors are trained to think a certain way, and, to the rest of us, that way of thinking is not always (or even often) a good way to think outside the medical field of diagnosis and treatment. But it's the way the doctor has been trained to think and respond, and you have to be prepared for it.

Based on their training, experience, and the way they're taught to think about everything from patient behavior to their own status as medical professionals, doctors are biased, too. When was the last time you enjoyed a good chat with your family doctor or specialist?

So, you have to know where the quicksand is when you're examining or deposing a medical doctor. One of the most common forms of "doctor quicksand" is the assertion that the practice of medicine is always extremely difficult. And it's hard to make the jury disregard that assertion. True or not, it will be a claim you need to counter.

One example comes from another case of undiagnosed kidney disease. It was a tricky diagnosis because the patient's test results looked very similar to results that would indicate a different rare and untreatable disease. Was the disease a glomerulonephritis kidney disease or light chain myeloma? (If the disease or condition is untreatable, there's no case for malpractice.)

Naturally, the defense anchored their case on this assertion that *medicine is difficult* and that there had been no way for the doctor to distinguish the test results indicating treatable kidney disease from those indicating this rare and untreatable disease. We had to roll up our sleeves and work hard to beat the argument in this particular case. *This is true (I swear): The defendants hired a doctor who called himself "Mr. Myeloma" to defend them.*

I had to do enough research to understand the different markers present in these lab tests myself, as there was no treatment for myeloma. Then, it was a matter of preparing my expert to be able to thoroughly and clearly explain to the jury the markers that showed the differences between these two diseases — without wading into the quicksand that all doctors often wallow in (describing all the patient's symptoms, detailing all the typical actions a doctor would take in response, et cetera).

Understanding how all the doctors in this case would be thinking, including the doctor who was my expert witness, was crucial to getting true justice for my client. I had to do real research into these diseases and be educated by my expert.

Correctly handling cases like this cost money — and a lot of that money is wisely spent getting educated by a brilliant expert. It was only after I knew the disease and how these doctors thought could I really prepare for them. And in this case, the preparation was essential to destroying their argument. Not only did we prove that my client did not have myeloma, but we also destroyed the defendants' expert testimony in the process. Mr. Myeloma swore this was an untreatable disease and a death sentence, and by his own calculation, my client should have died a year before we were in front of the jury.

Yes, he said my client should have been dead if he had this disease versus a treatable kidney disease that was misdiagnosed and resulted in end-stage kidney failure. Talk about lack of credibility! (Did I mention that we had our "dead" client wave to the jury at that point to show he was still alive?)

There's Quicksand Everywhere

As I've detailed, it's an uphill battle for the plaintiff's attorney in a personal injury case. There's quicksand everywhere (not just in the way doctors think and speak). Go to any room and yell, "CANCER!" People panic and assume the worst. Many cancers are totally treatable, but that is not the first thing average people (juries) think.

Of course, that's what makes winning cases like these fun and exciting. Win your case and get justice for David over Goliath, and you've really accomplished something. You've beaten the odds. And you've triumphed even though your opponents were smart, talented, and had all the advantages going in.

Other forms of quicksand you need to look out for:

The defendant might be highly regarded. Beyond the "doctors are heroes" bias, you might be up against a defendant who's adored by the community. In fact, your opponent's expert might be the doctor who's donating their fee to charity! You need to find out whether your opponent is highly regarded by the community and, as a consequence, your jury pool. Do your homework; don't fall into quicksand by finding out Goliath is a local hero during the trial.

The judge is probably biased against you. Again, do your homework, avoid the quicksand of learning your judge's predispositions the hard way (during trial). The overwhelming majority of judges in cases like these are former defense lawyers or people who have backgrounds working for big companies before becoming judges. They typically come from Goliath's camp! There are very few judges who come to the bench from Camp David (pardon the pun) or have worked on the plaintiff's side of the courtroom. We plaintiff's attorneys are too busy fighting for justice to run for judge, but insurance company law firms have time and money. Just be prepared!

Your local jurisdiction might be tight fisted. All that investment of time and money made by lobbyists, insurance companies, medical organizations, governmental entities, et cetera, pays dividends for Goliath in personal injury cases by creating incoming biases against plaintiffs. You'll surely run into at least some of that bias in every case. But you'll find that Goliath's stage-setting work has been more effective in some jurisdictions than in others, so if you're in a jurisdiction that's heavily predisposed against large awards, you'll want to know that going in. Again, do your homework, and do your best to avoid the quicksand. This is what we call "poisoning the well," meaning the available jury pool is already suspicious of your case before you start. Educate juries and be prepared for bias. Attack it head on in voir dire.

Your David has to be likable! Whatever other biases your jury brings to the case, they will likely want to reward someone they like. You can avoid some major quicksand during the trial by doing whatever prep and coaching you need to do to ensure your client comes across as a likable person. This is crucial. I've learned about this quicksand the hard way, and now I simply won't take a case if I don't think the client can come across in a likable way.

Recall the police-brutality case I mentioned earlier. No, the client hadn't deserved to be beaten up by the cops, but, coincidentally, he wasn't a good, likable person. If you want to be the "good guys" in court, you have to have a David who is, essentially, a good person!

There needs to be money somewhere from which a reasonable award can be paid. Remember, while it isn't about the money or "winning the lotto," money is the way we keep score in our society, and winning a sizable award is the only way your David can get justice. It's also the only way society as a whole can benefit through the financial punishment of bad actors and corner-cutting profiteers.

Check insurance. Verify that the defendants have the ability to pay when you triumph on your client's behalf. Finding out too late that there's no money available for an award is a particularly nasty form of quicksand you want to avoid.

I represented a family whose child had been born deformed because their obstetrician fouled up the delivery. It was a case of definite and demonstrable malpractice.

But the doctor had no money and (more importantly) no insurance.

No insurance, no money. No money, no justice!

We avoided this quicksand the only way we could: by bringing the hospital into the case and showing that their decision to employ an uninsured obstetrician who was poorly trained and poorly supervised made them culpable — which made the hospital responsible for the kind of award that would mean real justice for my clients.

Do your homework, avoid all the quicksand, and walk into the courtroom as prepared as you can possibly be. Thorough preparation leads to great confidence, and you should be supremely confident in your case for your David — because you're about to beat all the odds as you go about trying your case.

Be Prepared

Have I said this before? Good. Be prepared. Read for a day to speak for an hour. The worst of all quicksand is being unprepared. Know your case inside and out so that every available question or scenario is covered. (Yes, I know you are going to say you can't prepare for everything. But see how prepared I was for that comeback?)

When the judge or jury asks a question, be first to have the answer. When an expert says something wrong, jump right on it and correct them. If defense counsel misstates facts, be on them like white on rice.

It's the fun part of the job!

PART THREE

Trying Your Case

Chapter 9.

Create Your Story With Exhibits

I'm standing here in a small courtroom, and I realize that I'm completely trapped.

My case is solid — with my David well on the way to getting real justice, and the defense has no idea what's hitting them, so I don't mean "trapped" in that sense. What's trapped is me, physically, in a corner of this little courtroom.

Here's what happened: Years ago, I was working a case with my father, and we used an exhibit to powerful effect. It was a giant, white foam board, at least 8 feet long from left to right, on which we'd illustrated the timeline of the many instances the defendant doctor had seen our patient client (without coming up with the right diagnosis).

Well, when it was time to use the exhibit, I unfolded it and set it on the easel where the jury could see it. But the thing took up the entire space between the jury box and the witness stand. And as my father showed the timeline and explained the exhibit to the jury, I realized I was trapped back there behind the board. All you could see was this giant foam board with two legs sticking out from behind it.

After a while, it was becoming obvious to everyone that I had gotten myself into a ridiculous situation. I don't know what you would do if that happened to you, but the choice I made was to "limbo" myself out from behind the board, walk casually back to our table, and start taking notes as if nothing had happened.

Judging by the laughter, the jury was hysterical at this quite unintentional theatrical performance. It was embarrassing as hell.

But it was great because it became etched in the jury's mind. Not just the timeline or the foam board, but the entire event. As a result, my father referred to that exhibit repeatedly, saying, "Remember the board my son trapped himself behind?" Not "remember the timeline" or "remember the exhibit" — no. That exhibit became "the board my son trapped himself behind."

Embarrassing for me but *unforgettable* for the jury. And yes, we won, big time, and got some real justice for our client.

Using exhibits is not just about the information but about how you use the information and can get the jury to remember it (thus the point of this ridiculous story).

Mix It Up To Make It Memorable

Too many lawyers fall in love with technology and do everything with high-tech gadgetry, and I can understand why.

When you're using a computer and are a technical assistant (such as my assistant, Dan), you can move fluidly and quickly between pages of, say, a long document. "Dan, show page 4. Great. Now, Dan, show page 113. Thanks." And each page pops up on the wall or screen, larger than life, with the key messages highlighted.

That's the power of high-tech, audio-visual stuff, and there's nothing wrong with it. In many ways, it's great.

But if you use it too much — and we've all heard about attorneys whose entire case plan is to show these pages, over and over — it becomes like "white noise" and can lull your jury into a waking coma.

You can try asking the jury to "recall page 113" after days of this visual bludgeoning, but they probably won't be able to do so. Not like they'll remember "the board my son trapped himself behind!"

The key is to build your case through exhibits in a way that isn't too high-tech and isn't too low tech, but is *juuust* right. And that typically means mixing it up and using more than one methodology to display and explain your exhibits.

Someone in your jury might have recently sat through graduate school and been beaten to death by the high-tech visuals with which their professors had fallen in love. They'll likely find a foam board refreshing. More importantly, they'll *remember* the foam board.

I try to use "mixed media" in my cases whenever possible. I use Dan and a computer, but I also make giant foam boards. In some cases, what works best is a no-frills, old-school black-and-white document.

I use photos; I like to blow them up and display them larger than life on the wall or screen to maximize their impact on the jury. (Remember the "blow-up file?")

Sometimes, I use the old overhead projector with acetate-film slides. It creates a crooked, imperfect image that might be just the aesthetic I'm looking for in a particular moment in the case. I can also use a grease pencil to write on those slides to emphasize a point.

I even use a flip chart with a large pad of paper on an easel, and I write on it in my sloppy, nearly illegible style in real time, right before the jury's eyes.

Creating exhibits in real time can be very effective. For one thing, it shows that you (and, by extension, your David) have total command of the facts of the case; you don't have to rely on prepared exhibits but can actually illustrate key points for the jury in the moment.

When you write on a flip chart page or an overhead slide, it's almost like you and the jury are *creating* the exhibit together! And people tend to favor things they feel like they helped create. (Even if they didn't help create the page, they were at least present during its creation.)

And when you refer back to those words you've circled 50 times, it helps the jury remember the point. *Oh, yes*, you can almost hear them thinking, *I've seen this before.*

(Here's a helpful tip: Find out in advance what equipment will be available in the courtroom. Some rooms have screens, some don't, so you may have to bring one. Many have easels, but don't assume anything. Check it out beforehand.)

I bring a colorful little box to every trial, and I set it out where everyone can see it, almost like an elementary student who's proud of his new school supplies. My box contains markers, pens, sticky notes, a laser pointer, highlighters, rubber bands, paper clips, little flags, grease pencils for the overhead projector — everything I might need to create my case through visual aids.

Timeline exhibits are great, and I like to use different colors to create various psychological impacts on the jury. For instance, the timeline is in black before anything happens. It's red when disaster strikes, and it's green when the hero triumphs. The colors and media you use are just more choices you can make, and each deliberate choice becomes one more way to reach the jury (and even reach into their lizard brains).

And it all adds up over the course of the trial.

Blend the Visual With the Verbal

It's great to drive points home by anchoring your oral arguments with visual aids and vice versa.

A picture's worth a thousand words, as they say, so a picture plus the words are worth what — millions? It could be priceless!

Every image has a story. You show the picture; you tell the associated story. If you show the picture four times, then you tell the story four times, and the point anchors itself firmly in the minds of your jurors.

You might find this hard to believe, but I had a case in which the "star" visual aid was actually a little piece of rug.

Yes, *rug*. As in carpet.

The case involved the sad story of a man who had slipped and fallen off a stair climber machine at his gym, hit his head, and died.

Of course, the defendants argued that they had done everything they could to enhance safety and help prevent accidents just like this one. The defendant gym swore under oath that they had a unique safety system, engineered and tested for safety to protect against injuries. They had me depose their safety expert, who relied on this engineered safety floor to keep all Davids safe.

It took lots of time and effort, but I finally was able to get my hands on a sample of the safety-engineered flooring upon which the man had hit his head. It was a kind of thin, commercial carpeting, and it was *an 1/8 of an inch thick*.

You can't make this stuff up.

This thin carpet was glued directly to hard, poured cement. No pad, no buffer, just cement and a little piece of carpeting.

When I held up my little scrap of the rug and explained that it was not enough to put this much carpet over *solid concrete* and then say you'd done everything you could for safety — well, it was powerful. The "picture" had a story, and it was easy enough to put the two together in people's minds.

If a doctor failed to diagnose something, I want to show the jury what they missed. Remember the case where we helped the jury connect the dots by laying an X-ray image over an MRI to prove the cancer was in the same place where the bone broke? In cases like this, a good diagnostic slide or image can be very impactful.

I had another case of this type involving a cancerous tumor the doctor had failed to diagnose. I showed the image and let the jury see the tumor themselves. They could almost *feel* the tumor! And I anchored the image with a single word: *retrospect.*

Just like in the case where I associated "cognitive" with "brain damage," I used this image of the cancerous tumor to anchor the word "retrospect" by telling the jury the defense would use that word many times: "They're going to tell you that, in *retrospect,* you can see the tumor, but the defendant couldn't see it at the time. And every time they use that word, what they're really saying is that the doctor was wrong and made a big mistake but has a good excuse. And who among us lets our children get away with excuses, much less our doctors?"

A picture plus words equals justice in many cases.

Imagery can also help you appeal to the reptilian brains of your jurors in ways mere words can't.

Remember, your juror has core beliefs that form their personal *code*, and that code is embedded deep in their lizard brain. Identify the code, find the right words and pictures to appeal to it, and you'll be successful a lot more often than you'll fail.

I showed images at a trial involving a patient who'd suffered a badly broken bone in his leg. It would be more accurate to describe the bone as "shattered" into little pieces. The injury rendered the client unable to walk without a limp (forever), and I had the X-ray images to show it.

In voir dire, I found that a couple of jurors loved golf, just like my client did (though he was now unable to play). So I asked them what they loved about golf, and as I probed, I learned that it was really the *freedom* represented by the game — the fresh air, the outdoors, the relaxed pace, the fact that anyone can play just about any time they want — that my golf enthusiasts treasured.

I anchored the picture of the nasty fracture with the notion of a loss of *freedom*, not just to play golf but to do anything that involved a lot of walking or standing. "That's what's so bad about prison," I said, "You've had your freedom taken away. But while most people in prison got there by their own actions and choices, it was not my client's choice to be *imprisoned for life* by this injury."

I used the lizard-brain code differently in a toxic mold case by displaying images of a property that clearly showed dangerous toxic mold. But the landlord had failed to mitigate the problem because he didn't *believe* it was mold — even though the jury could clearly see that it was.

This landlord's core lizard-brain belief was that there couldn't be mold on the property, so he didn't *see* the mold even when he looked right at it.

But I was easily able to point out that the property could have been tested *scientifically* for mold, which would have prevented the problems the mold ended up causing. In so doing, I was accessing the jury's deep-seated code that *science is to be trusted*.

"Whenever the defendants say they didn't believe it was mold, what they're really saying is that they don't believe in *science* or in *health*, and they've taken away my client's health because of that disbelief."

You can imagine the favorable outcome we were able to achieve with this image, anchored to this simple story and related directly to the jury's underlying code of beliefs.

Less Is More

There's an old saying: "Everybody knows the Mississippi River … not everyone can name all the tributaries."

The point is that keeping things simple also makes them powerful. Dilute your case with an overabundance of exhibits and stories, and you'll likely diminish its persuasive power.

Focus on the story, educate your jury, and empower them with facts, images, and stories they can relate to so they can render a verdict that means justice for David and an improvement of their world. It's easy as one, two, three: 1) Help David (good guy), 2) punish Goliath (bad guy), and 3) help yourself (community) because you are worth the effort to be protected and safe.

If you can boil your case down to one powerful image attached to one powerful story, do it. The simpler you make things for your jury, the more they'll come to appreciate your case, your client, and your appeal for true justice.

Exhibits are key, but don't get trapped behind them — unless it works for you.

Chapter 10.

Select the Right Jury

We turn now to the MOST important aspect of trying your case. It's voir dire or (as it's commonly called) jury selection.

Parts of the trial process are more fun for me than others. Opening and closing arguments, for instance, are two of my favorites because I really get a kick out of finding clever, creative ways of delivering those arguments.

I love doing cross-examination, too. It can be very exciting (for me, anyway, though not necessarily for the witnesses). I'm also pretty sure the jury enjoys watching me fence in and destroy a bad expert witness or a doctor who's covering up the truth.

Other parts of the process are also important — critical, in fact — such as discovery and pretrial motions and lining up great experts and before-and-after witnesses.

But nothing is more significant than selecting the right jury to deliver justice for your David. You can win a "bad" case with a great jury. But a lousy jury can cost you a win in an otherwise fantastic case.

Knowing how to bring all your preparation and knowledge to bear in jury selection is often the crucial difference between getting true justice for David or letting Goliath get away with his gigantic misdeeds.

Selection or Deselection?

As Hamlet said, "Selection or deselection? That is the question!" (or something like that).

You can go into jury selection with the intent to select jurors who will help your case, or you can try to deselect folks who are likely to harm it. Many books have been written about jury selection and the different strategies and tactics employed by seasoned attorneys to get the right jury.

Either method (selection or deselection) can work just fine, but you should make a deliberate choice based on your preparation and instincts.

- Selection. Here, you're asking prospective jurors questions that reveal a bit about your case story, theme, and case rules. You're also looking for answers that help identify prospects as people who're likely to agree with your rules and, therefore, be helpful to David.

- Deselection. In some cases, your instincts might lead you to adopt a deselection strategy. Here, you'll frame questions around your case rules to find jurors whose lizard-brain codes are likely to lead them to disagree with you and think and decide in ways only Goliath and his giant army would. Your goal is to remove as many prospective jurors as you can.

Jurors Believe Other Jurors

It's essential to keep in mind that when you're asking prospective juror number 14 a question, *all* the prospects listen intently to both your question and their colleague's answer.

Use it to your advantage. One of the fundamental keys to success for your case is to get the jurors to *educate* and *influence* each other in the right way.

As you know, jurors often (almost always) come into the courtroom with a bias against attorneys. That bias is generally even stronger against YOU, the plaintiff's attorney, with jurors likely predisposed not to believe you.

Who *are* they likely to believe? Each other. Jurors are more likely to be influenced positively by other "average" people than by lawyers. And when they look around the courtroom, they'll likely perceive those seated with them in the jury box as the people they have most in common with.

Right away, during jury selection, you'll want to ask questions that give prospective jurors a peek at your case theme and rules, which will help you identify levels of agreement with those rules and probable points of empathy with your client.

An excellent way to assess levels of agreement is to thoroughly probe disagreement by asking "Why?" and by using "scale questions."

Suppose you ask prospective jurors whether they think a doctor should always check the lab tests they've ordered (alluding to one of your main case rules). In all likelihood, most will say they agree. But if one says they don't, you need to remember that all the other prospects heard that disagreement and are now waiting to find out why this other "average" person disagrees with what seems like a fundamental rule.

So, you have to ask them: "You don't agree that doctors should check the lab tests they order in every case? Why is that?"

"Doctors are heroes," your disagreeing prospect might respond. "They're busy saving lives and helping people. They don't have time for all that busywork."

"Busywork," you say. (Here's where you use the scale question.) "So, on a scale of one to 10, how often do you think doctors *should* check the results of lab tests they've ordered themselves, with one being never and 10 being every single time?"

Now you've got a good thing going. If the prospective juror gives a low number, like one or two, the other jurors might well decide that person's judgment is not as trustworthy as that of the rest of us average people. If they give anything above about a seven, the others might perceive that they're just a person who won't agree to an absolute but does fundamentally agree with your case rule. If they say, "It depends," you need to probe further with more "why" questions. In any event, you're using jury selection to start *educating* and *influencing* the jurors who will eventually be empaneled.

Build Empathy for David Into Your Jury

Think about who you want behind those closed doors, speaking to their fellow jurors during deliberation. You want jurors who will help you continue educating and influencing their peers in the direction of justice.

If you have a case involving a baby who died, you want moms and dads on that jury. It's unlikely you can get an all-parent jury empaneled (but go for it!) You just want enough parents with enough empathy to educate the rest of the panel on what it would be like to lose a child in infancy.

When you have a client who's a military service veteran, you'd love to have a couple of other vets on the jury. Or suppose your client owns a small business and has lost it (or lost revenue) as a result of Goliath's misdeeds. In that case, you'd love to have a couple of other small-business owners educating the rest of the panel about how hard it is to be the person who signs the paychecks.

You're looking for empathy for your client and using your jury selection questions to give and get information that helps you find those empathetic jurors (or deselect the candidates for whom empathy would be a stretch).

You're giving the entire prospective jury a peek at your case story, theme, and rules, finding out everything you can about them (and their biases) to use in rolling out your case. And since most jurisdictions have limits on how many facts of your case you can share during voir dire, you're getting your prospective jurors to do your work for you.

Remember, They Won't Tell You Everything

In fact, they can't. Most people who end up in your jury pool have built-in biases and codes going way back, and their lizard brains will influence their thinking and decision-making in ways they probably aren't even aware of.

But you really need to know what your jurors truly believe at the lizard-brain level. You need to uncover all the biases you can and use those in your trial, either by playing up helpful biases or de-emphasizing harmful ones.

Many prospective jurors dress up for court and appear eager, clearly wanting to present themselves in a certain way — usually as thoughtful, objective, and sincere. So they'll "self-monitor" to guard against revealing things they believe but don't want others to know.

It used to be an enormous burden to thoroughly probe and dig out these unspoken biases that govern jurors' thinking. But today (thank goodness), it's a lot easier.

Why? Two words: social media.

You can look up your prospective jurors on social media and find out a lot about them (including what they truly believe) by reading what they've posted, reposted, and liked.

Learning those things about your prospective jurors before selection even begins gives you a significant advantage. You can come into the process with your own predisposition on each prospective juror, either toward selecting or deselecting them.

For instance, if your client's a military veteran and you want vets on your jury, what if you find war-protest posts on a prospective juror's social media? Red flag, big time.

If your client is a small-business owner, you probably don't want someone famous for posting scathing no-star reviews online and who never has a good thing to say about the small businesses they patronize.

Learn everything you can about your prospective jurors, both before *and* during voir dire, and always be looking to select empathy and deselect adversarial codes.

Fight for It

You're up against it, as you know, given all the ways Goliath has the deck stacked in his favor before you even meet your David.

Sometimes, the rules of the particular court in which you're working or those of the judge before whom you're appearing are also stacked against you.

In some jurisdictions, you aren't even allowed to question prospective jurors during jury selection. The judge does that. All you can do is submit questions. (Hint: make sure you've done your online and social media research!)

And in many cases, your time is limited in jury selection. You always want to fight for as much time in voir dire as you can get. Make whatever appeals you can to the judge to get the maximum time permitted.

Whether you're asking the questions or the judge is asking them, you want to use those questions to give and get information, as described above. But when the judge is doing the asking, the formulation of your questions might be doubly important.

You're not supposed to make arguments or be specific about your case facts in the jury selection phase of the trial. But you better be as specific and revealing as you can get away with being! Otherwise, you're going to miss key bits of information about the jury's biases and codes.

Remember, your questions can offer prospective jurors a "peek" at your case rules, story, and theme. When the question is: "Do you believe doctors should check their own lab results?" it doesn't matter who's asking it; you've started to educate your jury pool about a crucial case rule and give them a hint as to what you're going to show Goliath did or didn't do for your client.

One more point: It doesn't do you any good to craft fantastic questions if you don't truly listen to the answers and, if you're allowed, question the prospective jurors yourself, probing those answers as deeply as possible. My advice to my fellow attorneys is the same as something I tell my kids: You have two ears and one mouth. Use them in that proportion! You should be listening twice as much as you speak, and while that's true throughout the trial, it's especially critical during voir dire.

Good Word Selection Leads to Good Jury Selection

Craft your questions to prospective jurors so tightly that every word counts — and choose those words for maximum psychological impact.

Unless you're doing it for theatrical and psychological effect, don't pause or use filler words like "kinda," "sorta," and "um" (the latter being a word only in a very loose sense). Use every word that helps your quest for information, omitting all others.

Another tip: Always refer to your client by their first name. It promotes affinity with the jury and portrays your client as one of them — just another "average" person who was simply minding their business (like the jurors do) before Goliath stomped nefariously into his life.

By contrast, *never* refer to your opponent by their first name. Make the defendant as *formal* as your client is *average*. Use their formal names and organizational labels, and portray them as exactly what they are: big, faceless, corporate manufacturing operations designed to make money, not "help people and save lives," as they might claim.

Bring to bear every little bit of psychological influence you can exert. Never put yourself in a position to look back and realize there was anything more you could have done to win your case or get more justice for your client, especially during this stage of the trial. You are a trial lawyer — a wordsmith — and a people person. Use your skills to connect, educate, and shape public opinion, as these are the fate deciders for you and your client. Remind the jury of the stakes involved and that they are there to dispense justice. For more information, I highly recommend reading "Gorgias" by Plato. In fact, it's required reading for all young attorneys who work for me.

You Start Winning Before Your Opening Argument

Jury selection is where you start the long march toward winning the case and getting justice, and you do that by beginning to nail down your case rules before the final jury is even empaneled.

Your voir dire questions "around" the specifics of your case will start to cement in the jurors' minds the belief that your case rules are solid and reasonable and that your opponent broke those rules.

In the case of my military veteran client who had suffered because doctors hadn't diagnosed his kidney disease, I started right away defining my rules and the doctor's missteps.

My voir dire questions actually helped set up my most important case rule: A lab result showing both blood and protein in urine indicates kidney disease *every time* without question.

Blood might enter the urine in a few different ways, as might protein, but when *both* are present in the urine, there's no doubt whatsoever about a diagnosis of kidney disease.

Before the trial got going, my focus group already had a firm grasp of my case rule, which had begun to form right away. I had handwritten charts with "B + P = KD" in large letters circled repeatedly. "Blood plus protein equals kidney disease." Even the focus-group judge started referring to "B and P"!

Making the jurors clearly understand this equation made things very difficult for the defense. They trotted out some lame stuff, such as pointing out that my client had "insurance issues" and was "overweight." But, at the end of the day, all that mattered was "B and P." And when I anchored that understanding, the focus group wondered why the defense was bringing up these other "distractions" and wasting their time!

Was there B and P in the urine or not? There was!

Then why are you spending all this time talking about insurance premiums and weight gain?

That one simple rule, combined with my case theme of "Veterans are heroes and deserve better than to be ignored by their doctors," led to an excellent outcome and justice for my client.

And it all started with the way I designed my questions and set up my case frame and theme.

The 10 Commandments of Jury Selection

To recap, you need to follow what I call the 10 Commandments of Jury Selection:

1. **Compose a trial story.** Start voir dire with a firm command of your story and with questions crafted to give prospective jurors a good peek at it.

2. **Elicit confirmation of your theme.** Use your questions to get information about your jurors and apply it to selecting jurors predisposed toward a fundamental agreement with your case's theme.

3. **Remember what you learn.** Whatever biases, codes, and beliefs you uncover during jury selection should be used throughout the trial. You have to keep coming back to them.

4. **Sequence your evidence presentation to align with the jury's codes and biases.** If you can start with a solid foundation using your case rules, it's much easier to unfold the case in a way your juror's lizard brain expects to be convinced!

5. **Heed the norm.** Remember, average people like norms. Get your prospective jurors to agree that "checking your lab results is the 'customary' way a doctor should do

business." And then, at trial, show that the defendant violated those norms.

6. **Reverse fundamental attribution error.** This starts right away during jury selection. Keep in mind that your jurors likely attribute heroism to doctors and deceit to "win-the- lotto" plaintiffs. Start reversing that right away with your jury selection questions. Don't allow prospective jurors to continue the narrative. Ask why they have certain opinions about your client and when they formed those opinions (and follow up). Remember, your client is righteous.

7. **Plan for hindsight bias.** The defendant is very likely to play up this bias, arguing that "anyone" could have made this mistake because no one has the benefit of hindsight. Your voir dire can anticipate this bias and begin to break it down in the juror's minds. Talk about what should be done in a normal situation with no further facts; then add a few facts and watch for the reaction.

8. **Create empathy.** Everything you do should contribute to a growing sense of affinity for David and a growing sense of discomfort with Dr. Goliath, who did not perform like the hero we expected him to be.

9. **Drop the anchor.** Start right away with things like "B + P = KD." Anchor your case rules as solidly as possible during jury selection.

10. **Close the frame.** If you've framed your case beautifully with a case rule like "B + P = KD," the defense will likely keep trying to pull the frame open. Always work to keep it closed. "B and P is the fundamental fact of this case. The defense's arguments about insurance issues and my client's weight are merely distractions designed to waste your time — and none of us should put up with that!"

Stand on Solid Ground With Case Rules

Typically, even the biggest case can be framed within the simplest of rules, such as, "You should always follow up," "You shouldn't hurt others," "You should always be safe," "You should provide a safe workplace," "Blood and protein in urine equal kidney disease," and so forth. And you can start laying the solid foundation provided by your simple case rules during jury selection.

I'm reminded of a case involving a transport truck driver whose job was to deliver a car to a dealership, and he ended up losing his life because the dealership failed to protect him adequately.

The dealership managers were concerned about possible scratches on the car this fellow was delivering (and, I suppose, on neighboring cars on their lot). So, instead of letting him park in the parking lot, they forced him to park his transport on the side of the road and unload there — where he was struck by traffic and killed, leaving behind a wife and children.

The defendants argued that he had been relatively inexperienced and hadn't used all the available shoulder to park the transport.

But my case rule was (of course) rock solid: The dealership had an obligation to provide this man with a safe place to do his job (unload cars).

My question to potential jurors gave them a good peek at the rule and helped anchor it firmly in their minds: "What would you say is more important — a scratch on a new car or a man's life?"

Given the power you have during jury selection to start framing and anchoring your case, along with the valuable information you can gather about your jurors and their codes during this early phase of your trial, you can see why I say nothing's more important than jury selection.

Get it wrong, and you're making an uphill climb toward justice much steeper — so steep that you may not be able to overcome it.

Get it right, and you're making things much easier on yourself in the long run. The 10,000 hours you spent reading and preparing was for this chance to talk to 50 or so captive people who are forced to hear you talk and watch your theatrics — truly a trial lawyer's dream.

Chapter 11.

Tell Your Story

Do a masterful job of unfolding your story for the jury, and you'll hopefully get what you came for: true justice for your friend David. Like I tell my clients, there are no guarantees with juries, but eight out of 10 times, they get it right.

(One time in 10, the jury awards "too much," and one time in 10, they go too low. These are the vicissitudes of trial practice, my friends.)

I can tell you for sure that experience is the best teacher. The more stories you tell, the better you get at rolling out an impactful story.

And, of course, if you test your story — with focus groups, in the bar, on the golf course, wherever you can tell it — you collect a treasure trove of information on which you can base your decisions on how to tell David's tale.

One word of caution, which lines up with some great advice I got as a young married man: Do you want to be *right*, or do you want to be *happy*?

In marriage, if you disagree with your spouse — even if you could be right 100% of the time — you'll never be happy if you insist on clinging to your rightness. (I always try to choose to be happy, but on occasion, I am dumb enough to forget my own advice.)

The same thing goes for the story you're about to tell the jury. You must tell it in a way that *confirms* what your jurors already believe, which you should be able to guess based on your jury selection and trial prep as it relates to their lizard-brain codes.

Insist on being right, in disagreement with your jury's lizard brains, and no matter how right you are, you will never be happy.

And neither will your David.

The Rhythm Method

No, not that one. I know I brought up marriage, but the rhythm method I'm talking about here is the art and science of taking advantage of the natural *rhythms* of your trial and your jurors.

Every trial and every jury has a rhythm. And if you're smart, you'll tell your story in a way that takes full advantage of that rhythm. We will discuss this rhythm more; needless to say, every witness testimony has a rhythm, every trial day has a rhythm, every story has a rhythm. For best results, tie into the rhythm of the day and the trial as much as possible.

An example of a trial day rhythm is a kidney case involving a treating pathologist who would not say what I wanted at deposition but instead hemmed and hawed for three hours. I videotaped the deposition.

I knew my own pathology expert was a great asset, and I needed to play the treating pathologist's deposition video to set up my expert's testimony. But I also knew the treating pathologist's testimony would not be helpful to our side.

So, to take full advantage of the trial rhythm, I waited until after lunch (around 2 p.m.) to play the video for three hours.

My experience has taught me that jurors are tired and sleepy in the afternoon after a big lunch. And to amplify this little factor, I'd asked for an extra half hour for lunch — so everyone would have time for a big meal.

I played the three-hour deposition in full, no cuts or breaks in hopes the jury would barely listen, and, sure enough, two jurors fell asleep!

Then, after a coffee break — when everyone was awake and alert and ready for the day to end — I put on my expert, who unsurprisingly closed the day strong. He left a lasting impression on the jurors, who barely seemed to remember what was said in the three-hour video.

Use your knowledge of the trial's rhythm to put together the case pieces in the order you want.

The 'Batting Order'

Once I've collected all the pieces of my David's story and tested the story several different ways with different audiences of "real people," the first thing I do is create a *batting order*.

People understand batting orders, and they appreciate them as much as they appreciate anything else in the wide, wide world of sports.

By the way, I can't say enough about how much I love sports. Maybe it's my background from the U of M (University of Miami). Go 'Canes! Maybe it's the Miami Dolphins, still the only

NFL team ever to put up an undefeated season. Maybe it's the then-Florida Marlins, who won the World Series as an expansion team or the decades of football greatness by my other alma mater, the University of Alabama. I don't know, but I *love* sports. They teach teamwork and fairness and give us all a sense of success and failure (and the opportunity to learn from failure).

I also believe sports make great leaders. I love to read about leaders and learn how they became leaders.

I have a quote on my desk, one of a dozen or so great quotes on display around my office, which says, "I never lose. I either win or learn." The quote is from Nelson Mandela, and it reflects what I truly believe. Sports, on the other hand, instill in us an understanding of the scoreboard. Jury verdicts and settlements are for the win but also teach us how to learn from defeat. For these and many other reasons, I use sports in my trials whenever I can.

So, once I've tested my story, I assemble it into a specific "batting order" (the order in which I'm going to unfold it for the jury). I align my witnesses, exhibits, experts, and every element of my story to this batting order, taking full advantage of what I know will be the jurors' rhythm during the trial.

Just as baseball managers want to put their most consistent hitters at the top of the order — the "cleanup hitter" in third or fourth position, the weakest hitters farther down the lineup, et cetera — I want to tell the good parts of my story when the jury is likely to be performing at peak energy and paying the most attention.

First thing in the morning, the jury's revved and ready. I put one of my best witnesses there. Late in the morning, when energy is flagging and folks are looking forward to lunch, I'll call a weaker witness.

Often, right after a quick lunch, when we've all had our coffee and our sustenance, and we're once again revved up, I'll put one of my stars up to bat at that time.

And late in the afternoon (when the jury's energy and attention are at its lowest ebb) is when I'll tell the part of the story that calls for playing a recorded deposition or something else that might put the jury to sleep — but might contain some less wonderful aspects of my story. So go ahead and snooze!

It's also important to bear in mind the principle of "primacy and recency," which says that the first and last thing the jury hears is what they'll remember most. So my "curtain ringer" might be to put the client's mother on the stand at the very end of the story. She can tell what a wonderful person her son is (or was) and give the jury a sense of David as a real, flesh-and-blood person — just like they are.

Everything has to be aligned. If I'm calling the medical expert, I need to have the associated exhibits showing X-rays or medical records. If I'm calling a personal witness to talk about how great my David is (or was), I'll have ready some personal photos that drive home my client's humanity.

And my exhibits align with my witnesses. When Mom is on the stand, I might pass around an 8-by-10-inch photo to the jury; whereas for my expert, I might project medical records from a computer screen for all to see.

You Don't Always Start at the Beginning

Once you've tested your story, you might realize that the most impactful way to tell it is to start at the end — "let's skip to the chase" — and then go back and tell the how and the why.

For instance, I told the story of a David who had suffered a horrible fracture and lost his ability to do one of his favorite things: play golf. (You might remember the case.)

I started, not with pictures of the fracture or the medical records but with the man's best friend. He took the stand and told the jury — in tears — how he hadn't lost his best friend (the man had survived) but had lost one of the things they most loved to do together.

My exhibit to accompany a witness like this might be a picture of the two friends hoisting a golf trophy they'd won together or pictures of the two of them playing in a golf tournament.

What next? The friend will only testify for 30-40 minutes, so I know I'll need to have the next chapter in the story ready to roll out. Should I go to the medical expert and the records or talk about how the doctors had missed the fracture?

In this case, the next logical step was to show images of the devastating fracture my client suffered. Once they saw those images, they fully understood what the doctors had missed and were fully primed to hear from the expert and digest the records.

And when the defendants started arguing that they had done "all they could" for the patient, their arguments mostly fell on deaf ears.

Every story's different, and each has a different natural rhythm and batting order. In the kidney disease case, my first witness might be the medical expert who can drive home the simple equation that $P + B = KD$. (Protein along with blood in the urine are absolute markers for kidney disease.) And if that's how I'm telling the story, naturally, the exhibits that help my expert drive home that point will be ready to go when they testify.

If You Do Nothing Else, Play to YOUR Audience

The most important aspect of telling your story is understanding and keeping in mind your audience. You *must* understand the people to whom you're telling the story.

For example, we would have learned in voir dire which jurors we really like for certain elements of the story. So, we'll tell parts of the story directly to those folks.

Not only does this create the maximum influence and impact on those favorable jurors, but it also arms them with what they need to make that part of the story clear to the other jurors during deliberation.

Keep in mind that a given juror *might* believe you if you're able to overcome the odds — but they're much more likely to believe a fellow juror.

In voir dire, when juror three says her dad's quality of life was the most important thing to her, look her in the eye and say, "This fracture is what took away David's golf life — and, more importantly, his quality of life he worked so hard for."

Remember the scoreboard? The way we keep score in this business is *money*. We need to tell our story in a way that drives the damages awarded to our client, not for the money itself, but for what it represents: true justice for David and the general betterment of our society as a whole.

Your audience (unfortunately for plaintiffs' lawyers) also includes a judge. This means you may need to adjust your batting order depending on the judge's schedule or the time it takes to conduct examinations. So be flexible. (Insert a mental picture of Mike Tyson here.) Even if you need to adjust your batting order, keep with the rhythm you want for the greatest impact on your audience (the jury).

Chapter 12.

Driving Your Damages: The 10 Commandments

Given that money is how you put points on the scoreboard for your David and the way you get justice (not just for your client but for society as a whole), you want to drive the damages to which your client is entitled as high as possible in the jurors' minds while staying within the scope of "reasonable and just."

There are 10 ways to do this. I call them the 10 Commandments of Driving Your Client's Damages. (Wow, that's another 10 Commandments! I need to think of a more original term to go along with 10.)

To maximize your client's damages and get true justice for your David, *thou shalt:*

1. Know the Law

This seems pretty obvious. But it's important to know that the laws regarding damage entitlements vary from state to state.

I had a case in Florida involving a man who was a bouncer at a popular Key West nightclub. He was a very well-known and well-liked member of the community.

The man died as the result of a *clear* case of medical malpractice: The emergency room personnel left him sitting in the waiting room so long with a severe nosebleed that he lost an incredible amount of blood and died.

He was single (though he did have a fiancé, which in Florida doesn't count) and had no children. As a grown man, he wasn't a "child" of his parents in the eyes of the court. So, by Florida law, there was no pain and suffering and virtually nothing to which this man's family was entitled.

I threatened to exert all my considerable efforts to get the law changed, and eventually, the defendants settled. But it was a paltry amount given the egregious harm they'd done this man and his loved ones.

The law is different in Hawaii, where I also have an office and do a fair number of cases each year. Hawaii places a limit on pain and suffering recovery, but there's no limit to providing for loss of enjoyment and happiness.

You might think that pain and suffering and loss of happiness and enjoyment are almost the same thing, and they are certainly closely related. But in Hawaii, you can't get a decent award if you're arguing pain and suffering.

In the case of misdiagnosed kidney disease in Hawaii, the client suffered immeasurably, but we succeeded in gaining a justice-sized award by pointing out that he'd lost his ability to live any kind of enjoyable lifestyle.

You have to know the law — along with what's possible (and what's limited) — in the jurisdiction in which you're trying your case.

2. Present Your Rule Violation

You've worked hard to establish your case rules: your undeniable, impossible-to-disagree-with rules of conduct and ethics, which should be the guiding principles in your case. Now you have to show how those rules were violated.

Another Florida case involved a man who worked as a roofer and was asked to use a foam epoxy to attach the shingles (rather than the old-school hammer-and-nail method).

The stuff was highly toxic, and the man got very sick from using it. His skin literally peeled off his hands.

The manufacturer of this ghastly stuff hadn't provided so much as a warning label to tell consumers about the risks associated with using it (possibly because printing a warning label would cost the company a little bit of money).

My case rule? Very simple. *Workers are entitled to be kept safe.* The defendant company had failed to do that. End of story.

The defendants finally agreed to my case rule, and they saw clearly how the company had violated it. We were successful in getting our David a sizable award.

3. Choose Your Words Carefully

Accidents happen, right? At least, that's the core belief your jury will start with.

So, in the case of a car crash, don't ever refer to the event as an "accident." It was "poor judgment" or a "dangerous choice" on the other driver's part.

The words you choose matter. Don't make a dangerous choice of your own by aligning your language with core beliefs that don't add up to a large award in your jurors' minds!

4. Focus on the Defendant's Conduct

We're seeking money, of course, since that's the only way we have to keep the "bad guy" accountable and gain justice in our system. But we're fighting more for what the money means: how paying it will motivate the defendants to straighten up and fly right.

I had a case where the state had let trees grow around stop signs so much that the signs weren't visible, causing terrible accidents.

We focused our case not on our client's collision but on the defendant's actions in letting these trees grow wild. We wanted a reasonable award for our client, but we wanted to drive the damages so the state would be motivated to go around to neighborhoods and make sure the stop signs (for which we'd all paid lots of money through our taxes) were visible.

That was our focus, and as a result, we got justice — for the client and all of us.

5. Concentrate on the Defendant's Motive

This tactic tends to be fairly easy in medical malpractice cases.

The hospital fired many employees to save money on salaries and benefits. Now, they've turned their facilities over to independent contractors and "hope for the best."

They made a choice motivated by money, and now it's going to cost them more than they saved as they have to cough up a huge award for David.

Focus on the defendant's motive, and you not only get justice for your client, but you often motivate real change in the defendant organization.

6. Establish That a Good Client Deserves a Large Reward

Juries want to help "deserving" people. So, if your client is a good, decent person, you should do everything in your power to point this out in court.

It's hard to take cases on behalf of convicted felons or people who helped cause their own damages because juries are not as eager to help them. So when you have a good client, make sure the jury knows it.

I had a *very* good client — well, my client was the man's family — who had been extremely successful in business and earned about $3 million a year. His family had a wonderful lifestyle but was also extremely philanthropic.

When the man was killed by medical malpractice, not only did the family lose a beloved member, but the community lost an important and generous benefactor.

At the outset, I prepared my voir dire to tell the jury I was just going to start with the fact that $10 million was simply not enough. This man would have earned at least twice as much if the defendants hadn't killed him, and the loss was great not just for his family but for everyone in town.

By the end of the case, the result was large enough for the family to live and still help their community.

Don't be afraid to mention money. It isn't a dirty word. It's just how we keep accountability and serve justice in our system.

7. Show That It's Not the Same as Winning the Lotto

The defendants will try to assert to the jury that you and your client are just bringing this action to "win the lotto" and grab a big sack of cash from their poor, heroic clients.

But it's easy enough to establish the case rule that no one would trade their health for money (not even lotto money).

When you ask a juror how much money they'd take for, say, their lungs or kidneys, it drives the point home pretty nicely. I have asked a jury to consider this very question. In closing argument rebuttal, after the defense attorney had claimed that the whole trial was about winning the lotto, I offered cash to buy jurors' kidneys to give to my client. When I asked the jury to put a price on their own kidneys, they realized that money is not the same as health.

We're not here to win the lotto. We're here to effect change and get justice for a deserving client.

8. Seek To Make Whole

Make the jury understand that it's not enough just to pay the medical bills your client incurred because of the defendant's misconduct and "dangerous choices." Simply paying the medical bills doesn't make your client "whole."

In most cases, it isn't possible to restore fully what your client lost — from the income they would have earned to the lifestyle they would have enjoyed. Your client may have had vital things taken away from them forever, such as the ability to fish or play golf or do countless other things that, to them, made life worth living.

And they have pain and suffering to boot!

But if the jury will grant them a large enough award, they might be able to retrain for a different job, learn a new hobby, or at least pull themselves out of suicidal depression and use some of the money to help them find a way to give their life new meaning.

To make a client whole means to pay all past and future medical bills; compensate for all past and future lost income; pay for the pain they endured and for their suffering (mental and physical); and compensate them for losing the enjoyment of life.

Think about that. Let it marinate. What is your price tag for giving up your ability to enjoy life?

That's often the closest the jury can come to making your client whole again after the defendants' misdeeds robbed them of a big piece of their life. And a sizable enough award might, again, provide the incentive for an organization to make real changes that keep the same robbery from happening again to someone else.

9. Don't Be Afraid To Ask for Money

Start your case by asking for money for your client … include that demand throughout the case … and end your story with it. Don't be the rookie lawyer who's afraid to ask for money.

In ancient societies, when you killed a member of my family, the only way I could get justice was to pick up my sword and go kill a member of your family.

These days, we're more civilized. We don't kill your family members — we use money as a way to give and receive justice.

It's a better system, and everyone understands that it is.

So never be afraid to ask for money. That's what you're there for, and the money award you're able to secure is really your only path to true justice in today's civilized society.

10. "Show That the Money Will Be Used for a Worthy Cause"

Remember the wrongful death case where my client's wife was killed when a ladder flew off the back of a Florida Department of Transportation truck?

The deceased woman was an epidemiologist and a college professor. And when her husband testified that he wanted to use a great deal of the money from the case to establish a scholarship fund for epidemiology students in his late wife's name, you better believe the jury couldn't wait to award a sizable sum and be part of that righteousness.

Even the government understood, realizing they had better settle for much more than the Florida cap in sovereign immunity cases to make us go away and start funding this new scholarship.

If you've got a good client who's willing to commit money from their award to a worthy cause, you absolutely *must* illustrate that fact for your jury.

You Must Follow These 10 Commandments (or Create New Ones)

I've presented the 10 Commandments of Driving Damages in order of importance, as I see them. But you should use every one of them in every trial.

Some will be easier to emphasize in your case than others, but you should bring every one of them to bear on behalf of your client. However, modesty aside, you may have developed better "commandments," so use those.

That's what great trial lawyers do! We take, we learn, and we improve. Be specific, narrative, and colorful (my favorite category). You know what you want, and your client knows what they want, and so should the jury.

Chapter 13.

Closing Is the Most Fun

You know, you work your tail off on cases like these because you're the only possible route to justice your David can hope to have. If you are really good, you take these cases (and your clients) to heart. You feel the pressure to do well — to help your client, help society, and be financially responsible to your firm. So you might as well also have a little fun in your career.

And that's where *closing* comes in.

Closing is the fun part. It's the reason you went to law school. It's the reason you studied so hard to pass the bar and become an attorney. Closing is the reason you spent all those hours preparing for trial — staying up all night reading through hundreds of pages of depositions until you could swear you felt little puffs of smoke curling up out of your eye sockets.

It's your payoff for putting up with all that crap from the judge when you were just trying to get documents entered. It's your reward for the patience you showed when the defendants and their Goliath attorneys treated you like dirt throughout the entire process.

Yes, closing is where you get to sit back, butter your roll, and enjoy the feast you've spent hours, days, weeks, months, and *years* preparing. Indulge yourself a little at closing and give yourself a chance to truly enjoy your work. It's what will keep you coming back for more; the Davids of the world are counting on that.

It's Your Time To Shine

At closing, you get to be the lawyer you always wanted to be. Want to be suave like Robert Redford or wicked-cool like Sean Connery or even entertaining like Nathan Lane? Do it! Be the very best version of yourself at closing.

This is your time — your time to *shine*! At closing, you get one to three hours to lay it all out for the jury, rolling through your entire story the way *you* want to tell it without interruption, objection, or argument.

You can use any exhibit, chart, document, or picture you want at closing. Use them all! You're not constrained by the rules of evidence that govern the other parts of the trial.

At closing, you have the jury's full attention — and, if you do a good job, you'll have them eating out of your hand. And you will have impressed your client; they will know they had their day in court.

There are very few rules or constraints when it comes to what you can do with your closing. You can be as theatrical or as brief and to the point as you want. You can pretty much do whatever you care to do. But what you *should* do, of course, is whatever your instincts and experience tell you will help drive the best possible outcome for *this* client against *this* Goliath from *this* jury, given everything you've established up to that point in the trial. No two cases are the same, and no two closings are the same.

It's All About the Big Picture

At closing, you're not making a speech. You're not pleading, begging, or complaining. It would be closest to the heart of the matter to say that what you're doing at closing is putting one to three *years* of preparation into the delivery of a *firebrand sermon*.

You're making it clear to the jury that your client represents *all of mankind* and deserves what we all deserve: fairness, justice, safety, enjoyment, prosperity, and whatever the defendants in the case have robbed (or tried to rob) from your David. How about the loss of the ability to enjoy life? What could be more meaningful than that?

And you're trumpeting the fact that the defendants have made poor, dangerous, ill-motivated choices that must be *condemned*. Their actions **cannot** be condoned! And any failure to condemn them might be construed as a tacit form of approval, quite possibly leaving the door open for the same tragic circumstances to befall the next "person like us," as represented by your client.

"The defendants need to take responsibility for their actions," you'll insist, "and you, the jury, get to make this clear to them."

At the end of your closing, your jurors should be practically cheering for your client and weeping at the immeasurable sadness of the wrong that's been done, not only to your David but to all of us, by this defendant's nefarious deeds and mistakes.

They should be hopping mad at Goliath and more than ready to demand justice for your client and society as a whole. The jurors should be relishing the opportunity to be part of a great correction in the world, ready to award damages at a level that should make it impossible for defendants like these to even *think about* doing these things to anyone else.

So preach it, baby. Deliver the sermon of all sermons. Pour everything you've got into your closing and enjoy the ride.

Let the people say, "Amen!"

It's Great Fun, but Closing Doesn't Do It All

One of the reasons closing can be so much fun is that, to some extent, the pressure is off. Closing is about tying everything together, but closing rarely is what actually sways the jury's opinions.

Everything you did up to that point will have influenced the jury. By the time you get to closing, jurors have their notes, and their minds are likely made up. And you've earned the right to have fun with your closing, to put on whatever show you want.

It's very hard to sway the jury at closing if you haven't convinced them by that time. But you can still put some points on the board.

I remember a case involving a client whose back had been badly hurt. This person had gone to three different doctors and received three different pronouncements about which part of the back was the problem.

The defendants tried to argue that this showed a remarkable inconsistency on my client's part, maintaining that they had given different answers when each doctor asked, "Where does it hurt?"

During the trial, I had used different colors on a chart to illustrate where each doctor thought the problem was and another color to show where the actual pain was located. As it turns out, the client had been remarkably *consistent* in reporting the discomfort; the doctors had blown it.

When it came time for my closing, I marched into the courtroom with my plastic-wrapped (to protect it) multicolored chart.

I whipped it out only to discover that the colors had all run and mingled into a brown blob in the sweltering Miami summer heat!

Undeterred and thinking fast, I heralded the chart and said, "You remember the blue! You remember the orange! You remember the green and the red! Well, now they've all run together to show you, conclusively and decisively, that the problem was always in one consistent place! This brown blob is the *pain*. It always has been the pain, and unfortunately, it will *always* be the pain. Brown is pain!"

It worked like a charm. But it wasn't this quick-thinking closing that convinced the jury. It was the work I'd done up to that point. All that prep allowed me to recover from an unexpected "meltdown."

As we'll discuss in the next chapter, your closing is just one more weapon in your arsenal as you go about "arming" your jury with what they'll need in their deliberations to find in your favor.

One more example of a fun closing: I had a client whose neck was badly hurt in a car collision but whose car suffered almost no damage. All the defendants really did in that trial was keep holding up their photo of the undamaged car and implying that my client's injuries couldn't be as bad as they were.

This was a tough case! My client really was hurt, but the car really wasn't, and it was quite challenging to make the jury see how both of these things could be true.

I ended up getting less than I wanted for my client (but multiples of what anyone would have thought that case was worth), and here's how.

At closing, I asked my opponent if I could borrow the photo of the undamaged car, of which they had been so proud. As you might imagine, they were only too happy to share it.

I then spent the next several minutes summarizing my case, but while doing so, I ran around the courtroom, whacking my open-palm hand as hard as I could on every hard surface imaginable. The jury box. My table. My opponent's table. The judge's stand. The court reporter's box. The wood-paneled walls. My table again.

I held up the defendant's car photo with one hand and whacked the courtroom with the other.

The judge was screaming at me. The jury sat in stunned, wide-eyed amazement and had no idea how to react. Even the court reporter kept screaming that they couldn't hear what I was saying over all the whacking and screaming.

After a few minutes, I held up my battered hand and asked the jury how much damage they thought I might've done to it — *internally*. Even though there was no apparent damage when examining my hand *externally*.

I sat down, my hand throbbing — it was killing me! — and a big smile on my face, at least externally. (On the inside, I was actually weeping with pain.)

The judge was mad at me, sure. And the jurors had been quite alarmed. But, as one juror told me later, it had been the most entertainment they had in a long time! And I certainly convinced them that there was almost nothing I wouldn't do to get justice for my client.

I had fun with my closing. And I had done the very best job I could do for my David.

Chapter 14.

Arm Your Jury

I've got some bad news for you if you're one of those attorneys who believes you are the most important person when it comes to persuading a jury to do the right thing for your client.

You're not the most important factor in that jury room when verdicts are decided. You're not going to persuade the jury in that room!

When it all boils down, the simple fact is that *jurors will be persuaded by other jurors.*

Even before the trial begins, you have too many things going against you to be the most influential person in the courtroom. The best you can hope for is to tap into the underlying lizard-brain code of *some* or *most* jurors, based on what you know about them, and *arm those jurors* with everything they'll need to persuade the others.

Once the jury's deliberations begin, they go behind a closed door, and your opportunity to influence them (or even talk to them) is over. At that point, you're hoping you've sufficiently armed your champions on the jury to fight for justice for your David behind that door.

Sometimes jurors will send questions out from behind the closed door. One of my favorites was this one: "Could we please have a calculator?"

Best. Jury. Question. Ever!

At this point in your copious study of this invaluable tome, the last thing you need is a repetition of the reasons you're really up against it before the trial even starts (and why a jury question like that one will always send you into a small bout of exhilaration).

So here it is:

- You have to work twice as hard (at least) as your Goliath opponents to prepare and present your case. For you, it's time-consuming, stressful, and expensive in ways it isn't for deep-pocket defendants. And, prepared as you may be, you can never anticipate everything.

- Judges are predisposed to dislike you (if not to hate your ever-lovin' guts). They typically come from Goliath's world, not David's.

- Jurors have been conditioned by insurers and other stakeholders to feel just about the same way judges do about you and your ever-lovin' guts. The defendants are "heroes," while you're just looking to win the lotto!

- Goliath and its attorneys have all the money and time in the world! You and your David? Not so much.

So you should be *thrilled* when the jury asks for a calculator. It probably means they're looking at a decent award for your client — which likely means that you've successfully influenced jurors to persuade other jurors who you would not have been able to reach otherwise.

Can You Read Tea Leaves?

If you can read tea leaves, palms, or, perhaps, palm leaves, you may have built the "muscles" needed to read juries.

Reading jurors is tough.

I can't tell you how many times a rookie plaintiff's attorney has tried to "read" the members of his or her jury, only to be flabbergasted by the results.

Remember, your job is not to persuade every juror. The best you can do is lay out a *boffo* case for the jurors you identified as sympathetic to your cause during voir dire and make sure those key influencers have everything they need to persuade the others. Do that, and your champion jurors will *fight* for you behind that closed door.

You'll use your case rules and knowledge of the "code" to speak directly to the lizard-brain *core beliefs* you discovered during the jury selection process and throughout the early stages of the trial. If you're successful, it will be because you presented your case in a way that aligned well with what your key influential jurors were already thinking and feeling before the trial even began.

A perfect example comes from a case involving an injured sea captain who lost the fingers from his right hand because someone had not tied off a rope correctly. The defendant shipping company argued this loss was the client's fault, as the ship's captain, and that he assumed the risk and had failed to monitor his crew on the charter.

The jury was sure to know the old saw: *The captain goes down with the ship* — meaning that the captain is in charge of every aspect of the ship's operation. So my entire voir dire was spent asking jurors about the authority to hire and fire. I found jurors who expressed frustration with co-workers they couldn't hire or fire.

Since the captain had been forced to accept the crew the charter company had hired, he had no actual authority. He'd been furious about the undertrained (cheap) crew he was assigned.

In this case, was the captain really in charge of every aspect of the operation? Not so much.

The jury felt the captain's anger and impotence and awarded him justly.

Make Everything Easy for Your Champions

It's critical you make everything your champion jurors need as *easy* as possible to take with them behind that closed door.

For instance, if your best exhibit was on a 6-by-4-foot board in the courtroom, make sure the jury has smaller copies they can carry back into deliberations. Also, make certain they can identify it in their "packet" as the same exhibit they saw during the trial.

This approach worked extremely well in the case I tried on behalf of the dancer who lost the use of her leg because a foreign car manufacturer had "cheaped out" on the steel they'd used.

In that case, the manufacturer handed over more than 100,000 pages of technical specifications (all in Japanese) for the car she'd been a passenger in. I finally persuaded the court to order the material be translated. Once that was completed, I sifted through the entire document (more than 1,000 banker boxes full of paper!) to find the two pages that prescribed the car sill should be constructed of "high-strength steel" (which, as you'll recall, it wasn't).

Those pages were star inclusions in my "blow-up file." Needless to say, I had them blown up onto huge boards for the courtroom. But I also made 8-by-10-inch copies for the jury.

That exhibit had been instrumental in showing the key elements of my story and case:

- By the defendant's own rules, the car should have been constructed of high-strength steel.

- My case rule, based on the jury's lizard-brain code: People deserve safe cars.

- The defendants' conduct: They took a leg to save a dime.

- The main rule violation: This manufacturer failed to protect my client (as they had a duty to do), and she lost her leg (and livelihood) as a result.

I'm happy to say we won justice for the client in that case; Goliath settled on the eve of the trial, after they saw everything I had during a 14-hour mediation.

Make Sure Your 'Why' Is Clear

In order to arm your champion jurors with everything they'll need to provide real justice to your David, you need to make sure they understand, above all, *why* you're in this fight.

And it isn't just for the money. The money is just a symbol for justice; it's no more than the points on the scoreboard.

In the case of the bouncer who'd died in the emergency room, we made it clear we were in the fight "so that no other mother's son will die of a nosebleed in this institution's care."

The jury of your client's peers will include people from all walks of life and likely include mothers and fathers.

Mothers *fight* for their babies.

Parents *fight* for their children.

Siblings *fight* for life.

Retirees *fight* for the ability to live on their own terms.

Students *fight* for health.

So when you illustrate your client's "why" to your influencers on the jury, you're tapping into the juror's core beliefs and helping your case resonate with them.

Bottom line: Think through everything you've used during the trial, and make sure you've done everything possible to arm your key jurors with the ammunition they'll need to fight for you in deliberation with the other jurors.

What you do is important. It's true. But what you do to arm your champion jurors — and what *they* end up doing to influence the other jurors — is the most essential element in your case for justice.

"Do unto others …"

Conclusion

How David Beats Goliath

Over the years, our legal profession has developed into a modern system that has created, essentially, two types of lawyers: the business lawyer and the advocate lawyer.

Business lawyers have excellent systems for making money through the representation of clients in such matters as medical malpractice, personal injury, and product liability. Their business-focused practices actively seek clients for whom they typically gain settlements. When their firms are successful, it's because they're representing a *lot* of clients and making a *lot* of money in legal fees, as represented by a good percentage of those settlements.

They run expensive ads to get lots of clients, and they make lots of money from those clients' cases — so they can afford to run more expensive ads, et cetera.

That's fine with me. But it's not what my practice is about.

I'm an advocate lawyer. My "system" is not so much about making money, though we've been very successful over the years for our clients. My system generates *true justice* for the Davids of this world against the Goliaths who've wronged them.

My system seeks to make a difference in people's lives, the laws of the land, and the conditions in which we all live. As such, it isn't really a "system" at all, but a certain tried-and-true methodology for getting that justice — one client, one case, and one trial at a time.

Each "David" is different from another, and each case must be handled individually and with great care. That's pretty much the definition of "advocacy," and that's what MY practice is all about.

I hope you've enjoyed (and learned from) "How Justice Is Served." We've covered a lot of territory from years of "trial"-and-error refinement (get it?), all of which resides in a giant binder I call my "trial book." It contains notes that represent every scrap of learning I've been able to assemble over many years of hard work in trying righteous cases for the Davids I've represented.

As an advocate trial attorney, you'll develop your own "secret sauce" when it comes to getting justice for your clients. You might even be building your own trial book." I'm hoping this volume will help you add to your system and abbreviate the time and effort you'll put into developing your way of doing things.

Have you picked up some good ideas for evaluating, preparing, and trying your cases? Have you learned a thing or two about overcoming the odds by assembling a winning theme, a set of case rules, and a story? Are the tricks of the trade in "How Justice Is Served" useful to you?

If so, I hope you'll encourage your colleagues to read the book and reach out whenever they come across a David who needs an advocate in court. (If not, I'd appreciate it if you'd keep it to yourself.)

Just remember that there are many forces and organizations promoting themselves every day as caring and compassionate but don't really give a hoot about the Davids of the world. Employers, insurers, even corporate money mills disguised as hospitals and medical practices — they don't care about your clients.

Only you do. You're David's last line of defense. You *must* help justice get served!

But that doesn't mean you can't enjoy what you do and do the very best job you can. Adopt that advocacy philosophy, and it's never a job.

It's a privilege.

Jed Kurzban Esq.
305-444-0060
Jed@KKTPLaw.com

About the Author

Jed Kurzban, Esq., brings more than a quarter century of experience in legal practice, along with an overstuffed "trial book" of notes and learning, to the authorship of "How Justice Is Served."

Mr. Kurzban has been an equity partner in the highly esteemed law firm of Kurzban, Kurzban, Tetzeli & Pratt for several years, concentrating his practice on trying plaintiff cases involving medical malpractice, product liability, and personal injury. The substantial awards he's secured for his clients over the years demonstrate his dedication to using his skills as a trial lawyer to help good people get justice — and effect lasting positive change in the world.

He's AV rated by Martindale-Hubbell, was elected to Super Lawyers by his peers, and has been named by the American Institute of Personal Injury Attorneys as one of Florida's 10 best attorneys. Jed is admitted to the bar in Florida and Hawaii (as well as the U.S. District Courts in Southern and Middle Florida and the Eleventh Circuit Court of Appeals).

Mr. Kurzban graduated from the University of Alabama and received his law degree from the University of Miami School of Law where he taught a pretrial litigation course.

He's enjoyed a prestigious academic involvement in addition to his professional practice, having led law school courses and co-authoring academic journal articles, such as "It Is Time for Florida Courts To Revisit Gooding" and "Offers of Judgment: The Current Minefield."

Jed is a foodie and a sports fan. He lives in the Miami area, where he grew up, with his wife, Lorna, and their children, Elspeth and Ailsa. Jed continues to try cases around the country, and with the support of his partners Ira, John, and Helena, he continues to fight for the Davids and swings for the fences.

References

Ball, David, and Don Keenan. 2013. "REPTILE in the Mist (and Beyond): The Plaintiff's Attorney's Guide to the MIST-Case Revolution." New York: Balloon Press.

Friedman, Rick, and Patrick Malone. 2010. "Rules of the Road: A Plaintiff Lawyer's Guide to Proving Liability." Portland: Trial Guides, LLC.

Expert
Press

www.ExpertPress.net